Sex Without Guilt
In the Twenty-First Century

Sex Without Guilt
In the Twenty-First Century

Albert Ellis, Ph.D.

Fort Lee, New Jersey

Published by Barricade Books Inc.
185 Bridge Plaza North
Suite 308-A
Fort Lee, NJ 07024

www.barricadebooks.com

Library of Congress Cataloging-in-Publication Data

Ellis, Albert.
    Sex without guilt in the twenty-first century / Albert Ellis.
       p. cm.
    Includes index.
    ISBN 1-56980-258-0 (pbk.)
    1. Sex. I. Title: Sex without guilt in the twenty-first century. II. Title.

HQ31.E624 2003
306.7--dc.21

                                       2003048140

Manufactured in the United States of America
First Printing

Dedication

Dedicated to the countless men and women who have fought the lonely battle against guilt for doing sex acts that are neither harmful to themselves nor to others.

Also dedicated to Debbie Joffe, who helped me enormously with this revised book.

Contents

Acknowledgments

I want to acknowledge the many people who helped me with this book, especially Patrice Ward, Ariana Ruiz, and Tim Runion. Many thanks!

Original Introduction for Sex Without Guilt *in 1958*

I first became aware of what *The Independent* was and what it stood for in the winter of 1955, when Paul Krassner, who was then its managing editor, and who later became the editor and publisher of the uniquely iconoclastic periodical, *The Realist*, wrote to ask if I had any unpublished material in which they might be interested. He had become aware of my work in the field of sex, love, and marriage and family relations, Paul said, when he had read my book, *The Folklore of Sex*. Did I, he asked, have any articles which other periodicals had refused to print, but which *The Independent*, which he managed, might be delighted to rescue from obscurity?

It just so happened that I did have several censored articles on sex; and after reading a few issues of this unusual monthly newspaper, I was more than willing to submit them to *The Independent*. This periodical, which I had previously heard about, struck me as being utterly unique in its field—a truly non-partisan publication with no axe whatever to grind except one that is perhaps the least seldom wielded in our presumably democratic nation: that of absolute, complete, and unequivocal free speech.

The more I got to know about *The Independent*, and to become familiar with the work and personality of its publisher and editor, Lyle Stuart, the more did I realize that perhaps never before in the annals of American publishing has anything like this paper existed—or at least flourished so persistently and well. Other liberal periodicals have, of course, existed—and some still do. But almost invariably, these publications have beaten the drum for some political, economic, or social point of view.

Not so *The Independent*. Its one avowed purpose was to print anything of legitimate and significant news value that is not easily publishable elsewhere. And by anything I mean anything. While politically liberal periodicals frequently have religious or sexual taboos, and while socially enlightened journals often have political or economic prejudices, *The Independent* was the only paper in 1956 that had *no* taboos or restrictions, and that published *all* kinds of news and fiction, no matter on whose political, economic, religious, medical, sexual, or other toes its contents stepped upon.

This is not to say that I always agreed with the editorial or other matter in *The Independent*. I didn't. Its columns, like those of all liberal periodicals I know, were sometimes devoted to exaggerated or over-scarily presented attacks on certain vested interests, such as the American Medical Association, whose activities I was not enthusiastic about, but which I did not judge to be as nefarious as some of *The Independent's* writers did. It also published a series of articles attempting to whitewash the notorious Krupp dynasty in Germany, whose viewpoint neither I nor the editor endorsed.

That, however, was the uncommon virtue of *The Independent*: it printed views, including many of my own, that Lyle Stuart by no means personally favored but that he nonetheless felt should be given a public hearing. Perhaps there are several other modern publications that more than occasionally do this, too. If so, I cannot at the moment recall them.

In any event, my reading of several copies of *The Independent* induced me to send Paul Krassner four papers that I had written on sexual topics for which I could find no publishing outlet. All these papers had been commissioned by other periodicals or book publishers, and were eagerly awaited by the commissioning editors. They were all quickly rejected, however, accompanied by apologetic notes or phone calls which explained that although they were clearly and interestingly written, their subject matter was too uncompromisingly sexual for them to appear in public print. When resubmitted to other publications, their content was still found undesirable for modern mass media.

Shortly after I sent these four articles to Paul Krassner he wrote me that he had shown them to Lyle Stuart and that they both felt that these were just the thing for *The Independent*: they would run them all. So they did; and so much reader interest was thereby engendered that, starting with the February 1956 issue, I became the paper's regular columnist—the only sex columnist, I daresay, writing for any American newspaper at that time.

My road as a columnist for *The Independent* was not totally unrocky. Thick and fast comments on my commentaries began shortly after I began writing, and all were hardly favorable. Of the more than thirty letters regarding my articles that were first published in the paper, almost two thirds were savagely negative. Icy salutes, for example, such as these:

From a man in Harper Woods, Michigan: "Please cancel

my subscription at once. It is not the kind of reading matter we want to have coming into our home. With all the important matters to write about nowadays, you publish some nonsensical stuff; especially that article on masturbation."

From a correspondent in Daytona Beach, Florida: "Dr. Ellis is a materialistic hedonist of a low-grade Epicurean type. I say 'low-grade' because the classical Epicurean was more discriminating and restrained in his search for pleasure."

From a woman in San Francisco: "It seems pitiful that a young man such as you [Lyle Stuart] should delude yourself that you are doing mankind a service in printing all the foul mouthings of men who have been unable to break into print elsewhere."

From a man in Phoenix, Arizona: "The sexual behavior material is bound to attract attention, particularly from deviates and those of the gray world, but is hardly suitable for including in *The Independent* just because no one else will publish such tripe."

From a woman in Topeka, Kansas: "Discontinue my subscription. Your articles by Albert Ellis and other features are absolutely vile."

From a virgin in Lancaster, Pennsylvania: "That sex article [Adultery: Pros and Cons] is absolutely hideous. The writer of your article should be in jail. I wish to tell you I am a virgin. After my mother died, two men at different times wished to marry me. So don't get the idea I was forgotten. The decision to remain a virgin is my business.

"Furthermore, as pertains to that horrible sex article, I wish to tell you I believe in the King James version of the Bible from cover to cover. It says: You dare not commit fornication or adultery. God have mercy on Dr. Kinsey and the man who wrote your sex article...."

And so on and so forth. Considering that *The Independent* was decidedly a liberal paper, that it was sold mostly by subscription, and that its readers were generally well educated and enlightened, it is somewhat surprising that so much antisexual sentiment was provoked by my monthly column. Not that the anti-Ellis letters were necessarily typical of reader reaction: since, from long experience with publishing controversial material, I have found that people who oppose one's views are more likely to write excoriating letters to the editor, while people who approve are likely to write directly to the author or, more commonly, to keep their favorable opinions to themselves.

Nonetheless, I think it significant that so many of *The Independent's* readers, most of whom were probably men and women of good will with liberal attitudes on a host of politico-economic issues, became embarrassed and angrily red-faced when confronted by reasonably liberal sex views. This is not the first time I have noticed that some of our most violent and virulent "radicals" are, at one and the same time, proper prudes.

The detractors of my *Independent* sex articles, however, have not entirely monopolized the field. My own files include a good many letters from favorable correspondents, and Lyle Stuart told me that he met many Ellis fans who never bothered to write me or the paper. Included in *The Independent's* published letters on the Ellis controversy were these:

From a female psychology student: "The article on masturbation is worth the subscription price for a hundred years. It is so normal and natural an explanation."

From a man in Chicago: "Am very much pleased with the articles Dr. Albert Ellis has been presenting in your paper. I have long been impressed by the fact that he is one of the very few psychologists capable of being honest all the way with society."

From a correspondent in Whittier, California: "Ellis... is a man not afraid to tell the truth."

From a professional worker in Portland, Oregon: "I am still pro-Ellis.... May he keep up his good work of presenting the facts of life rather than the reflection of what the moralists think things should be."

From a man in Boulder, Colorado: "I especially appreciate the articles by Dr. Ellis, and that they are undoubtedly undeleted and unchanged from the way he submitted them."

From a correspondent in Ridgefield, New Jersey: "Here are four hearty cheers for your Albert Ellis articles!"

From a man in Cleveland, Ohio: "I am a pro-Ellis enthusiast, and I agree with Dr. Ellis whole-heartedly that when it comes to sexual hypocrisy, we Americans are its greatest champions."

Evidently, from the tone of these letters, the lynch-Ellis coterie was not entirely in the saddle. Vociferous, yes; but not quite unanimous. And among the most loyal supporters of my right to print heretical sex views, if not always a supporter of these views themselves, was Lyle Stuart, who reaffirmed his faith in free speech in an editorial which appeared in *The Independent* at the time many cancellations were being received because of my columns on premarital sex relations. Lyle wrote:

"Dr. Albert Ellis writes about sex matters. Although he is prominent in his field, some of the things that he has written in some of the articles were not allowed to appear in books that he authored or in papers that he read before learned societies.

"Does that mean that we approve of everything Dr. Ellis

writes? Not at all. It means that we approve of Dr. Ellis's saying what he wants to say, frankly and without censorship."

The controversy raged up to the time I wrote my final regular column for *The Independent* in 1960. A woman in Sun Valley, California attacks: "I am increasingly ashamed to have your paper brought to my mailbox. I would not have believed it possible to publish such material as the Ellis articles in the United States." And a wife in Yoder, Wyoming replies: "We like *The Independent* as it is, including the articles by Dr. Ellis. Why don't those who object to them just ignore them? Can't resist them, I'll bet. And then they are so-o-o shocked!"

Meanwhile, I continued to go about my nefarious business, turning out pieces on sex, love, and marriage for one of the few periodicals in America that would uncensoringly print them.

Here, then, are the still unbowdlerized articles that appeared in my eventful two years as *The Independent's* columnist. Some of them, which were continued in two or three successive issues of the paper, have been consolidated into single chapters; and others have been somewhat augmented, because of the more liberal space allowances available between the covers of a book.

Introduction for the Twenty-first Century

I was happy to see, when I started to bring *Sex Without Guilt* up-to-date for the twenty-first century, that almost all the chapters required little revision. My uncensored views of 1958, I still largely hold today. A few chapters were somewhat out of date, so I have either omitted or revised them or replaced them with materials from some of my more recent writings. I mainly tried to stick to my original theme—that it is quite possible for readers to have a wide variety of sex-love acts, many of which are banned or censored in America and Western civilization, and not damn their behaviors or, especially, themselves.

As this book—like the original edition of *Sex Without Guilt*—tries to make clear, certain sexual (and non-sexual) acts needlessly harm yourself and/or others, therefore can be viewed as "wrong," "mistaken," or "sinful," had better be discouraged and avoided, and lead to feelings of self-censure and guilt if you engage in them. Think about this. See if your sex-love thoughts, feelings, and acts are *really* "harmful" and "bad" to you and/or others. If so, try to change your self- and other-defeating relationships. But Rational Emotive Behavior Therapy (REBT)—which I start-

1

ed to use and teach in January 1955, three years before I compiled the first edition of *Sex Without Guilt*—teaches you that even when you perform a harmful and wrong sexual (or non-sexual) *act*, you are never, never a bad *person*. I demonstrated how you can achieve this kind of unconditional self-acceptance (USA) in the first edition of this book. I am delighted to bring this view up-to-date in *Sex Without Guilt In the Twenty-first Century*.

As I said in the first edition of this book, if this be sexual heresy, please make the most of it!

Albert Ellis
Albert Ellis Institute
45 East 65th Street
New York, NY 10021
aiellis@aol.com
August 2003

1

New Light on Masturbation

Although attitudes toward masturbation have become more liberal during the past few decades, it is still rare for many writers on sex to take a wholly unequivocal stand on it. The point is continually made that masturbation is not as bad as it was once said to be; but the important point that it is actually good and beneficial is often not stated.

Censorship of outspoken articles on masturbation is still common, but was unusually popular when I talked and wrote against it in the 1950s. In fact, the original version of this chapter was refused admittance in a book which I edited and in a scientific journal of which I was associate editor; and when it was given as part of an important symposium on religion and sex, the entire symposium was never published.

At this same symposium, several prominent psychologists and psychiatrists objected strenuously to my statement that masturbation is quite harmless by pointing out that it is sometimes accompanied by neurotic fantasies. They did not, of course, stress the fact that, quite frequently, heterosexual coitus is also accompanied by neurotic fantasies.

3

We might do well to take another look at the problem of masturbation and try to see it in a more realistic light than that which is usually shed on it. It should come as no surprise, of course, that Dr. Alfred Kinsey and his associates found that about 93 percent of their male and 62 percent of their female subjects masturbate at some time during their lives.

It is perhaps more important, however, when they inform us that the female tends to reach orgasm more easily and quickly by masturbation than by any other sex technique; that it is much the most important source of sexual outlet for the unmarried females studied; and that females who masturbate have a considerably better chance of achieving orgasm after marriage than those who do not. This has been found again by several recent sex surveys.

As any serious student of sex knows, it is virtually impossible for most human beings to suppress their biological impulses completely, and if these impulses do not show themselves through so-called "normal" manifestations, they will frequently take "abnormal" forms of outlet—including neurotic symptoms.

One would think, therefore, that a society such as our own, which often opposes premarital and extramarital sex relations, would welcome masturbation as a convenient, discreet mode of sex activity that makes it possible for almost any person, if he or she wishes, to have a satisfying orgasmic release when most other forms of sex outlets are barred. In this respect, our own society is blind and destructive, for not only does it often ban all sex outlets except marital intercourse, but it also discourages masturbation.

Not that matters in this respect are as bad as they used to be. Not quite. But where old-time sex books promulgated an honest Puritanism that was forthrightly anti-masturbational, modern manuals are often subtly and more dishonestly antisexual in this respect.

A communication, for example, from the staff of the Child Study Association of America, consisting largely of trained psychiatric social workers, tells us that certainly masturbation "does not lead to blindness, brain fever, impotence, or any other physical or sexual ill-effects." The Child Study Association staff then goes on, however, to point out that because children in our culture do learn that masturbation is dangerous, and consequently become guilty about it, "perhaps the best course is for parents reassuringly to ally themselves with the child's own conscience in this matter and while assuring him that the practice will not harm him, also help him to find ways to grow out of it."

A more pernicious attitude than this could hardly be found. Essentially, it is the old puritanical view on masturbation brought in again by the back door after it has ostensibly been kicked out of the front.

Obviously, if children do get the idea that masturbation is dangerous, they get it from someone; and if this idea is a false one—as it most definitely is—it preferably should be solidly contradicted, instead of being cowardly accepted and perpetuated. Actually, the "dangers" of any sex activity by children and adults and the endorsement of complete abstinence from these dangers, is shown in detail in Judith Levine's unusually courageous twenty-first century book, *Harmful to Minors: The perils of protecting children from sex*. Read it and see!

In non-sexual areas, no one, and certainly not a group of clinicians, would ever make an equivalent mistake by discouraging masturbation. Many children believe, for example, that breaking a mirror, failing to knock on wood at certain times, or passing in front of a black cat is dangerous, and become anxious when they engage in such activities. Are we, then, to ally ourselves with these children's misled ideas and try to help them grow out of breaking mirrors or passing in front of black cats? Or are we not, rather, to show them how silly their fears are and how effectively to overcome these *superstitions* instead of stopping the *actions* leading to their fearfulness?

So with masturbation. Of course, in our inhibited culture, children learn that masturbation is dangerous and become guilty when they engage in it. All the more reason, then, to disabuse them of this fear, and to teach them to thoroughly accept masturbation—as an undangerous, beneficial human act.

Similarly with the other neopuritanical notions regarding autoeroticism which clutter many of our sex education texts. Let us, once and for all, say the final scientific, clinically based nay to these anti-masturbational notions. Some of the main quibbles that we may demolish are these:

The objection that masturbation is immature

Masturbation is not in the least an immature, adolescent sex act, but is just as mature as any other mode. As Kinsey showed, in unmarried college level males between the ages of 26 and 30, masturbation provides 46 percent of their total sex outlet; and in women between 36 and 45 years of age, 54 percent of the single, 36 percent of the married, and 58 percent of the previously married subjects admitted masturbating. In view of these facts, to call masturbation an immature or adolescent activity is to ignore the facts of human sexuality.

Masturbation may be "abnormal" when people who have a choice of several other outlets, such as heterosexual or gay sex in addition to masturbation, can *only* experience masturbatory satisfaction. Such people are rare. Virtually all other individuals who masturbate, at whatever age, masturbate *and* enjoy other sex acts and are "normal."

The objection that masturbation is unsocial

The idea that masturbation is a lonely, unsocial habit that leads people to avoid the company of others because they satisfy themselves sexually is highly questionable. It makes as much sense as the notion that going to a movie is socially healthier than viewing television at home or that people who read at home are poor lonely souls while socially healthy persons read in libraries.

A man or woman who is unsocial and who fears facing others may well masturbate instead of trying to achieve heterosexual relations, but rare is the individual who becomes unsocial *because* of masturbation. About *guilt* over masturbation, yes; but not over masturbation itself.

Sex behavior that most encourages isolation seems to be total abstinence, including abstinence from masturbation. If moralists wish to minimize human loneliness and unsociability, they had better look at people's fear of rejection and their low frustration tolerance about the trouble of making social contacts. These anxieties, as I show in *How to Control Your Anxiety Before It Controls You* and *Feeling Better, Getting Better, and Staying Better*, interfere with socializing. Not masturbation!

The objection that masturbation does not lead to full emotional gratification

The idea that masturbation is condemnable because it is an act which is incapable of giving full emotional gratification is a notion that is, at best, partly true. In the first place, many people, particularly those with good fantasizing powers, do obtain what to them is emotional gratification from masturbating.

7

Secondly, no sex act—including intercourse—can, nor for that matter necessarily should, give full emotional gratification at all times to all people. The idea that every sex act, in order to be "good," must be intensely emotionally satisfying, and that sex without love is evil, is a puritanical notion that I consider in chapter 5.

The Kinsey Report and other studies show that women do not necessarily *need*, though they enjoy, good partners or love relationships to achieve satisfying orgasms. What they require is consistent friction and pressure to the most sensitive parts of their genitals.

It may well be, therefore, that much of the romanticism and emotionalism women are *supposed* to have for sex satisfaction is largely invented. Men, of course, can obviously and easily masturbate to orgasm with little emotional involvement. In any event, the idea that masturbation is not emotionally gratifying and that it therefore cannot lead to satisfactory sex is largely mythical.

The objection that masturbation is sexually frustrating

Although masturbation, for many people, is not as sexually satisfying as, say, coitus, it is by no means always frustrating. When it is frustrating or emotionally unsatisfying, it has often been *made* so because individuals in our culture are raised to *believe* this "fact."

A man or woman who has been reared with anti-masturbational attitudes will often find self-stimulation unsatisfactory. One who has been raised with liberal attitudes will normally find it quite satisfying—though not, usually, as much so as sex with other people.

The objection that masturbation leads to sexual inadequacy

Although it has frequently been held that autoeroticism leads to sexual problems in males, there is no data to support this allegation.

The notion that female masturbation conditions women so that they cannot enjoy coital satisfaction is contradicted by the Kinsey researchers, who found that among the females studied who never masturbated to orgasm before marriage, 31 to 37 percent failed to reach coital orgasm during the early years of their marriage, while among those who had masturbated before marriage, only 13 to 16 percent were coitally unresponsive in the early years of marriage. My own clinical experience also shows that many women are definitely helped to achieve satisfactory marital relations if they first engage in masturbatory activity.

The objection that masturbation may lead to sexual excess

The idea that masturbation is likely to be taken to excess is another puritanical myth. As has been noted for many years in sexological literature, the erotic response, in both males and females, depends upon a remarkably foolproof mechanism. When people reach their physiologic limits, they no longer respond erotically. The male becomes incapable of having further erections; and the female, though able to have intercourse, does not enjoy it.

Only a disturbed person would masturbate when he or she had no desire, and might consequently do so to "excess." A normal individual's actually engaging in "excessive" masturbation is rare.

Altogether, then, the attitudes on masturbation that still fill some of our sex books, attitudes which state or imply that autoeroticism, while not completely harmful, is still not "good" or "desirable," have no scientific foundation and constitute a modern carryover of old antisexual moralizings.

The facts are that the vast majority of American males and females engage in a considerable amount of masturbation, and that, particularly in view of our other restrictions on sexual activity, they would be abnormal if they did not.

It is difficult to conceive of a more beneficial, harmless, tension-releasing human act than masturbation that is spontaneously performed without (puritanically-inculcated and actually groundless) fears and anxieties. Let us, please, now that modern authorities have stoutly reaffirmed this fact, see that our sex manuals and sex education texts unequivocally say it in plain English.

Actually, masturbation is usually a harmless and quite beneficial sex act, as many twenty-first century sex manuals are beginning to unashamedly assert. Look into, for example, Bernie Zilbergeld's *The New Male Sexuality*, Sari Locker's *Amazing Sex*, Steve Salerno's *The Book of Sex*, Alex Comfort's *The Joy of Sex*, James R. Petersen's *365 Ways To Improve Your Sex Life*, and Betty Dodson's *Orgasm For Two*, as well as, of course, her *Sex For One*.

Some distinct advantages of masturbation include the following:

1. It has saved innumerable single and mated, straight and gay people from stressful abstinence when they, for one reason or another, were denied sex with other people.

2. It has warded off an enormous amount of anxiety, depression, rage, and low frustration tolerance that many sexually deprived people would have felt if they had not resorted to it.

3. It has promoted sexual fantasy and imagery throughout the world, much of which has aided interpersonal sex relations.

4. It has saved a great many mated relationships when one or both of the partners were not receiving enough sex satisfaction with the other partner.

5. It has promoted the invention of satisfying kinds of sex that would have not been created had people not resorted to masturbation.

6. It can be used to enhance the sex enjoyment of partners, as Sari Locker shows in *Amazing Sex*.

7. Mutual masturbation is an important part of foreplay and afterplay in heterosexual and gay relationships. It can work beautifully when one or both partners is unable to reach orgasm in coital sex. Betty Dodson says in *Orgasm For Two* "the electric vibrator is to women what Viagra is to men."

8. In the case of many women, self-stimulation or masturbation by a partner is almost the only means of their reaching orgasm.

9. As Betty Dodson notes in *Sex For One*, it is harmless and can be totally acceptable for children. It often aids their later sex life. Alex Comfort, in *The Joy of Sex*, adds that masturbation is one of the best experiences that a "man can use at any age in learning to slow down his response to a level which gives the woman a chance." He also states that masturbation is an important process of continuing self-exploration than it is in men, "and many women can and do teach themselves to respond in this way."

10. Anne Hooper wisely points out in *Sexopedia* that masturbating a partner to arousal and orgasm differs widely for individual partners. Therefore, considerable practice with *your* partner will often bring both of you to the most satisfying results.

11. Mutual masturbation not only includes caressing and

manipulating a woman's main sex organs (e.g., her clitoris and vulva) but also other parts of her body (e.g., her G-spot, if she has a sensitive one). For a man, it not only includes various kinds of manipulation of his penis by his partner but also stimulation of other sensitive parts of his body (e.g., his nipples, his scrotum, and his prostate gland).

12. People's aging does not stop their ability to benefit considerably from masturbation. Hilda Hutcherson in *What Your Mother Never Told You About Sex* reports the case of a 73-year-old woman who had never had an orgasm and who, after Dr. Hutcherson's few weeks of instructing her how "to stroke, massage, and discover the areas of her sexual anatomy that brought her the most pleasure" experienced "glorious orgasms." Apparently, it's never too late!

2

Thoughts on Petting

Like masturbatory activities, petting generally has a bad name in our society. It has been variously claimed, by authorities as well as laymen, that petting for its own sake or petting to the point of orgasm is abnormal, perverted, unhealthy, immature, frustrating, and frigidicizing. Is there any truth to these allegations? Virtually none.

Let us start our discussion of petting with a few essential definitions. By petting we usually mean sexual stimulation of another person that is done for its own sake rather than as a prelude to intercourse. It may or may not culminate in orgasm for either or both of the partners. It largely consists of contact with your partner's body, particularly her or his erogenous zones; and it is usually done through caressing, embracing, kissing, biting, and massaging. When it includes mutual nudity or direct stimulation of the genitals, it is often called *heavy petting*.

Sex literature often condemns petting, but most of this applies to prolonged petting that does not lead to orgasmic release. According to some authorities, such non-climax-producing petting may result in tension, pains in the groin, headaches, and other physical discomfort.

13

On the other hand, it would appear that literally millions of individuals, especially great numbers of women in our society, are able to engage in prolonged petting sessions with no harm and with real satisfaction and tension reduction. For these individuals, petting for its own sake is more beneficial than avoiding all sex relations. At the same time, it can be suspected that many of these women would derive still greater benefit from petting to orgasm.

Petting to climax appears to have no serious disadvantages when compared to actual coitus. It may not be as pleasurable as is intercourse, particularly for the male; but, on the other hand, many people, especially women, find it even more satisfying than intercourse.

Petting to climax involves, in all the major details, almost exactly the same kind of excitement and response as does coitus. This is particularly true when it involves petting a woman's clitoris or vaginal petting, with the male entering his partner's vagina with his fingers instead of his penis. As far as can presently be determined, most men and women experience the same kind of orgasm through petting as they do through copulation—providing that they do not have some significant psychological prejudices favoring one of these two kinds of sex.

When it is practiced exclusively as a means of achieving orgasm, petting may be a form of sexual fetishism. Thus, it may be exclusively resorted to as a means of sex because a person is phobically afraid of having intercourse.

Petting to orgasm is particularly normal and healthy when it is resorted to because other forms of sex relations might result in difficulties. Thus, if two people want to have sex and want to make sure that they avoid pregnancy, they can safely obtain virtually all the satisfactions they want without having to take any risks. Or if two individuals can only have sex relations in a semi-public place—such as a parked automobile—and wish to minimize the danger of detection, petting may be more practical than coitus.

It is most surprising—as Dr. Alex Comfort has pointed out in his book, *Sexual Behavior in Society*—that a culture such as our own, which frowns so heavily on premarital sex relations, and particularly stresses the dangers of premarital pregnancy and abortion, should also disapprove of petting to orgasm. For young people often have strong sex desires—and if they are determined to have some kind of sex, it would seem far wiser to encourage them to pet to climax rather than, say, to have premarital coitus.

Our own society, alas, is neither perceptive nor wise in this connection. It frowns upon premarital intercourse—as well as on thoroughly undangerous sex acts, like petting. In so doing, it virtually ensures that youngsters will frequently have intercourse when, if they had more rational sex education, they would do much more petting to orgasm. A most peculiar paradox!

In any event, petting itself would seem to be rarely harmful when it is carried on in its own right, and quite harmless when it is carried to the point of mutual orgasm. The vast majority of males and females can easily come to climax through various types of petting; and there seems to be no good reason why, when they want to, they should not.

Sex conservatives, of course, point out that if we ban youngsters from having *any* kind of sex, they will not heavily pet and risk the danger of having "dangerous" intercourse. Maybe!

What are some of the distinct advantages of petting when you engage in it purely for its own sake (yes, even without you or your partner coming to orgasm) or when you add other enjoyments (including orgasm without

15

intercourse and intercourse itself to your petting activities)? Here are a sample of its sex-love benefits:

1. Only after a good deal of experimentation with being properly (or "improperly"!) petted are many women able to reach orgasm. Men with retarded orgasm also require considerable petting experience to be able to come.

2. Both sexes, including gays, often require petting experience and experimentation to bring their partners to orgasm efficiently.

3. Coming to sex heights by your partner's hand (or mouth or other parts of his or her body) is often distinctly better than by self-stimulation.

4. Petting that includes being stimulated orally (including oral-genitally) is one of the best desserts a partner can supply. The Redbook *Report on Female Sexuality* found that 90% of women found oral sex enjoyable. A similar report on men's enjoyment of different kinds of oral sex would have probably shot up to 98 percent!

5. A main way to a woman's heart and sexuality, found Lena Holstein and many other authorities, is through opening her sensual—and not merely her sexual—door. Ditto with men! The strong taboos of our culture that condemn children's touching themselves may impede their natural sensuality for the rest of their lives. Unless they later contradict this taboo and engage in considerable self-touching and partner-touching.

6. Steve Salerno recommends that considerable petting can be—and is!—done in planes and trains. The blankets issued on planes can be used for warming your

body—and for covering your sexual warmth! Plane and train toilets can also be used for sex privacy.

7. Heed Alex Comfort in *The Joy of Sex*: "Skin is our chief extragenital sexual organ—underrated by men ... better understood by women."

8. Petting is called *outercourse* by Dr. Hilda Hutcherson. Fine! Remember that, like intercourse, it often culminates in beautiful orgasms—in the case of many women, of course, *more often* than intercourse. But men, too, can often come to climax by petting when intercourse is not quite feasible or just doesn't work that well.

9. If you want to learn about a number of unusual ways to enhance your sex life by petting (and also by coital techniques), try browsing through James R. Petersen's *365 Ways To Improve Your Sex Life*. But watch your becoming obsessed with sexual techniques!

3

The Case for Premarital Sex Relations

A good number of books on sex and marriage relations discuss the pros and cons of premarital intercourse, and wind up by being against it.

Few of these texts, however, give an adequate discussion of the issue, since they list, with no grain of salt, many "disadvantages" of fornication that apply to the 19th century and 20th century, rather than today's America, while failing to list many advantages of premarital affairs.

A more sophisticated and fairer presentation of the pros and cons of sex before marriage is not often published in these United States; and when it is, it certainly isn't widely circulated in school and college courses on sex-love etiquette. Yet, all the facts at our disposal show that premarital relations have been unusually widespread in America for the last four centuries.

Just for the record, it might prove interesting to make a fairly complete list of the advantages and disadvantages of sex behavior among the great American unwed. First, let us list, and with some degree of critical judgment appraise, the alleged evils of premarital sex:

The dangers of venereal disease

Although uninformed people still are fairly frequent victims of VD, the infection rate among well-educated individuals is low. With the proper use of prophylactic devices, on the one hand, and modern antibiotics on the other, the informed person who engages in premarital sex activity has little chance of suffering severely from a sexually transmitted disease (STD). Betty Dodson, with over 40 years of "promiscuous" sex behind her, has never had an STD, and I personally, who have "screwed around" with some 40 women during the last 66 years, have only suffered from two cases of nonspecific urethritis, which lasted for a short while. Great luck!—or due caution in my choice of sex partners.

"Illegitimate" pregnancy and abortion

Modern methods of birth control have been so well perfected today that so-called premarital pregnancy and abortion are rare among those who carefully and consistently employ easily available techniques. Again, though my fertility has been normal (until I had a prostate operation and a vasectomy 20 years ago), I have never impregnated an unmarried woman in my many years of premarital (or adulterous) sex.

Guilt and anxiety

Since premarital sex relations are no longer viewed as sinful by most educated and informed individuals, you need not suffer intense guilt if you have them. People who are anxious and guilty because of their premarital affairs are usually also anxious and guilty about many of their non-sexual doings. On the other hand, many people today become anxious and depressed because they are *not* having sex before marriage.

Loss of reputation

Today's young people, including women, are rarely severely condemned or ostracized for their premarital adventures. On the contrary, they are as likely to lose the esteem of other youngsters for remaining virginal. People who greatly fear any loss of reputation because of their premarital proclivities are often disturbed and could use psychological treatment such as Rational Emotive Behavior Therapy. They usually create for themselves a dire need for social approval, which REBT has helped to reduce in many cases.

Sex inadequacy

While it used to be feared that individuals having premarital affairs would tend to be sexually deficient in their later life, all reliable existing data tend to show the opposite. The more premarital sex activity a young person has, the more is he or she likely to be sexually adequate in his or her later life, including married life. Many studies, including those of Alfred Kinsey and William Masters and Virginia Johnson, have found this.

Emotional risks

Although it is true that people who engage in premarital affairs take risks, in the sense that these affairs may break up and they may thereby be pained, it is also true that young people who love each other *without* sexual involvement take similar risks, and may just as easily be saddened. Besides, taking risks, and being disappointed in some of the things one does, are hardly necessarily harmful to people, but are part of the process of emotional growth and development. Youngsters who take *no* emotional risks are much more likely to become seriously disturbed, as I have shown in many of my books on REBT.

Exploitation of one's sex partner

Exploitation of one's sex partner generally occurs when one individual (usually the male) has sex relations with another under false pretenses—pretending that he loves her or will marry her. Such exploitation doubtless occurs in premarital affairs: not because of the affairs themselves, but because of the dishonesty of the people engaging in them.

Where both partners, moreover, frankly have sex relations for sexual (as well as other) satisfactions, such exploitation is reduced to a minimum. Consequently, the more open, honest, and frequent premarital intercourse tends to become, the less potentially exploitative it remains.

Sabotage of family life

It has often been alleged that premarital sex relations sabotage family life and keep people from marrying and raising healthy families. There seems to be no scientific evidence to support this belief, and much contrary evidence that tends to show that individuals who have premarital sex experience marry more easily, and are more relaxed about raising their children (and especially educating their children sexually) than those who remain abstinent.

If premarital affairs really destroyed family life, the human race would have long since died out, since young people at many times and places have had considerable premarital sex.

Sex without love

Premarital intercourse, it is alleged, leads to sex without love. This is nonsense, as most of the great lovers of human history, such as Heloise and Abelard, heavily fornicated. Sex, no matter how it is indulged, often creates and enhances love.

Virginity, especially when it is prolonged, seems to be the true enemy of love. Sex without love, moreover, is hardly a heinous crime. Rather, it appears to be quite delightful and adds immeasurably to the lives of literally millions of individual, as I have shown in chapter 5.

Sordid surroundings

Premarital intercourse, it is said, is often performed hastily, in sordid surroundings, under the fear of discovery and other poor conditions. Perhaps this was so in the nineteenth century; but the vast majority of today's premarital acts are performed in places and under conditions which are often just as good (and far more romantic and exciting) than those existing during marital relations. And they are usually arranged so that fear of discovery (or any great to-do about actual discovery) is minimal.

Lack of respect for partner's conviction

It is contended that those who have premarital sex often do not respect their partners' convictions against such relations. This is drivel. In our society, very few persons *force* or *coerce* another to have intercourse with them.

One partner may well talk the other partner out of his or her prior convictions against sex activity; but surely this is just as legitimate in sex as in politics, religion, or any other field where people have convictions.

Lack of responsibility

It is often objected that those who fornicate obtain all the pleasures of sex without any of the responsibilities of marriage. But why, if that is what they want, shouldn't they? Couples who date platonically, or love each other without sex relations, or who play tennis together also obtain satisfactions without assuming any of the responsibilities of marriage.

Why *must* everyone marry to be a good citizen?

And, even assuming that most people will eventually marry, why should they marry and assume responsibilities with *every* person they are sexually attracted toward, fall in love with, or want to have as a tennis partner?

Subsequent adultery

It is said that those who have premarital affairs are more likely to engage in adultery after marriage. Granted that this may be so, it has never been shown that those who have premarital sex engage in considerable adultery after marriage, nor that they were adulterous because of their premarital affairs, nor that their adultery destroys their marriages.

On the contrary, there is some evidence that adultery may aid, save, and stabilize a marriage because, if it were impossible to have it, more people might feel driven to divorce!

Suspicion of adultery

It is contended that if people have premarital sex, they will then keep suspecting that, after marriage, their mates have adulterous affairs with others.

This is simply not true: for the majority of those who have premarital sex relations (which means the majority of people now marrying in America) rarely keep suspecting their mates of adultery—except, of course, when they have some cause to do so.

Partners who suspect their mates of being adulterous merely because they had premarital sex relations tend to be insecure and disturbed themselves—and often can use psychological help.

Lack of happiness in marriage

It has been reported in several studies that individuals

who have premarital sex relations are less happily married than those who are virginal at marriage. This finding may be specious because people who have premarital affairs are more adventurous and risk-taking than those who marry as virgins. They therefore may more honestly face and risk divorce if their marriages don't work out well.

Clinical evidence tends to show that people today who have premarital sex relations are just as happy in marriage than those who do not.

Promiscuity

It is often held that if an individual has premarital sex relations he or she will become promiscuous. This is simply not true. The majority of men and especially women who have had affairs before marriage have had them with relatively few individuals and have been very far from promiscuous.

Indeed, exceptionally few people in our society are ever really promiscuous, since promiscuity means lack of discrimination in choosing sex partners, and it is the rare person who is really indiscriminate in this regard.

When promiscuity really exists, it may stem from (a) unusually high sex desires and capacities or (b) emotional disturbance. These are hardly likely to *result from* premarital sex but often may be a *cause* of such relations.

Unachievable ideal

It is sometimes held that premarital sex relations are often so satisfying and premarital affairs so free and adventurous, that marriage suffers by comparison and cannot easily compete with this lovely ideal. This may sometimes be true. But if people did not have premarital affairs, the relationships that they would consequently *imagine* would be even more glamorous and adventurous than marriage and would serve as unfair comparison to it.

25

Many people can only tolerate marriage because they have, in practice, seen the disadvantages as well as the advantages of having affairs before marriage. The more affairs they have, the more realistic they may be, and the more likely they are to accept the restrictions of marriage.

The foregoing alleged limitations of premarital sex are not exhaustive, but would appear to cover the main points that are commonly raised about it. As can be seen by my rebuttals, none of these objections had too much validity in the first place or, if they were once true, applied largely to conditions existing many years ago.

Today, the same objections do not apply to the mentally healthy and educated people who have premarital affairs. Obviously, seriously disturbed and ignorant people will usually have more sex and marital difficulties because of their limitations whether or not they have premarital sex.

I shall now outline the other side of the story—the advantages of premarital affairs. This is the side that is conspicuously absent from many published writings on the subject. There are many obvious benefits to be derived from sex before marriage. Here are some of them:

Sexual release

Most human beings require some form of steady sexual release for their maximum healthfulness, happiness, and efficient functioning. If these individuals are not married—which many millions of them, of course, are not—the best form of relief from sexual tension they may obtain is probably through premarital sex.

Psychological release

In many, though by no means all instances, individuals who do not have premarital affairs are beset with serious psychosexual strain and conflict and tend to be obsessed with sexual thoughts and feelings. These individuals can often be considerably relieved of their psychosexual tension if they have satisfactory nonmarital affairs.

Sexual competence

In sexual areas, as in most other fields of human endeavor, practice makes perfect and familiarity breeds contempt for fear. In the cases of millions of unmarried males and females who are sexually inept, there is little doubt that if they engaged in steady relations before marriage, they would become definitely more enlightened and competent!

Self-acceptance

Although, as noted in the first section of this chapter, engaging in premarital affairs involves distinct risks, especially the risks of being rejected, there is almost no other way that people can enhance their self-acceptance and desensitize themselves to emotional vulnerability except by deliberately taking such risks and learning how to healthfully react to sex-love failures.

Avoidant male and female virgins in our culture usually often *confirm* their fears of rejection.

Adventure and experience

A rigorous restraint from premarital affairs leads to neutrality or nothingness and a lack of adventure and experience. Particularly in this day and age, when there are few remaining frontiers to explore and unscaled mountains to climb, nonmarital affairs furnish a prime source of sensory-esthetic-emotional experimentation and learning. Good! See chapter 15 in this book on Sexual Adventuring.

Improved marital selection

Because marriage, in our society, is usually infrequent

and long-lasting, people who marry should preferably have the kind of knowledge and training that will best help them to make a good marital choice. Among the very best experience they can acquire is to have one or more premarital affairs and, through these affairs, be able to discover much relevant information about themselves and their partners.

Moreover, people who engage in premarital sex are able to wait until they are in a good psychological and socio-economic condition to marry; while if they have no such affairs, they often feel impelled to make a rash and poorly selected marriage because of their sexual deprivation.

Sex democratization

The maintenance of premarital virginity, particularly among females, tends to encourage a double standard of sex morality and discrimination against equal rights for women. Premarital affairs tend to break down this auto-cratic, anti-female attitude and promote democracy and equality between the sexes.

Decrease in jealousy

Violent jealousy of men and women is largely the result of banning extramarital affairs and viewing one's mate as one's exclusive property. This kind of jealousy would prob-ably be distinctly reduced if a more liberal attitude toward premarital affairs was promoted.

De-emphasis on pornography

The increasing emphasis on the female form and on pornographic presentations that is currently so widespread in our culture is encouraged by our restrictions on pre-marital sexuality. The more people engage in satisfactory premarital relations, the less they will be inclined to be interested in second-hand picturizations of sex.

Savings in time and energy

Considerable time is wasted in our society by people constantly *seeking* sex gratifications in the path of which we place unusual obstacles. Persons who actually engage in steady premarital affairs save this kind of wasted effort and considerably enjoy the time that they do devote to sex activity.

Reducing discrimination against single people

Many people in our culture for one reason or another do not care to marry or are in no position to do so for the present. There is no reason why they should be discriminated against *sexually* merely because they are nonmaritally inclined.

By permitting these people to have premarital affairs, we would reduce discriminations against single people. As things stand, however, many such individuals who had better not marry or procreate are driven into unhappy matings because they desire sex outlets.

Sexual varietism

Many people strongly desire sexual varietism, especially during certain periods of their lives. A practical way for these persons to fulfill their desires is through premarital affairs.

Limiting prostitution

Whenever premarital sex on a voluntary basis becomes more common, prostitutional relations tend to decrease. If prostitution is deemed to have distinct dangers and hazards, a good way to decrease these would be to encourage premarital non-prostitutional affairs.

Reducing abortion, single parenthood, and venereal disease

If premarital sex were accepted, it would be a relatively simple matter to minimize the danger of abortion, single parenthood, and venereal disease. By allowing premarital affairs we could much better reduce some of the dangers that, because of puritan bolstering, still are common in such affairs.

Reducing sex offenses

Most sex offenders, as shown in my book, *The Psychology of Sex Offenders*, are not overly promiscuous individuals with wide-spread experience. On the contrary, they are usually inhibited, constricted persons with relatively little sex experience. If these individuals would engage in more frequent, more satisfying premarital affairs, many of them would commit fewer sex offenses.

Sex is fun

As has been previously noted by myself and others, sex is fun; straight and gay sex is often the very best fun; and more sex is still more fun.

Assuming that people who remain virginal till marriage are more pure and saintly than those who do not, we can hardly say they are commonly happier and more joyful. To fornicate may be "sinful"; but it is also a rare delight. We could well work at making it less rare rather than less delightful. Again, see chapter 15 on Sexual Adventuring.

Lack of responsibility and commitment

Some people are allergic to responsibility and/or commitment—not only in sex and love but in work, school, sports, and other affairs. This may seem to be a real lack on their part, since if they were more responsible and committed, they might enjoy life more intensely. But there is no reason why they *must* be serious and devoted to what they choose to do. If they can find a sex partner—or more than one—who doesn't mind, or even likes, their lack of commitment, let them. Why should we try to force them—probably futilely—to be "normally" committed? Let them be!

This, then, is a nonexhaustive list of some of the main advantages of premarital sex relations. Such a list does not indicate, of course, that it is good for all persons at all times under all circumstances. Obviously, it is not.

Many unmarried people, for instance, may prefer not to engage in sex mainly because the risks of pregnancy, however slight when proper precautions are taken, still do exist. Others may decide to refrain from heavy petting because they would then tend to become too emotionally involved with their partners, and prefer not to be so involved.

There are certainly good reasons why, in some instances, some persons may prefer to be abstinent or may only engage in petting rather than intercourse. The relevant question, however, is not: *Must* a healthy person engage in premarital affairs? It is rather: *May* an informed and intelligent individual in our culture justifiably and guiltlessly have sex before marriage?

On the basis of the existing evidence, viewed quite apart from the myths which are so widely published and broadcast, it is exceptionally difficult to see why he or she may not.

The average American has 6 to 13 sex partners, mainly between the ages of 16 and 24, outside of marriage. If premarital sex were totally unavailable, it looks like at least half our population would have to stick only to masturbation or total sex abstinence. Pretty grim!

4

Adultery: Pros and Cons

We have now considered the pros and cons of premarital sex relations and concluded that it is difficult to see why well-informed and reasonably well-adjusted young people in our society may not justifiably engage in such affairs.

The question now before us is: Should we reach the same conclusion about adultery? More specifically: Granted that, for a variety of reasons, adultery was hazardous in former times, and that the biblical commandment, "Thou shalt not commit adultery" *once* made some sense, is the case against extramarital relations still valid *today*?

We can see, at the outset, that many of the old grounds for opposing adultery are just as senseless, in today's world, as many similar grounds for combating premarital sex affairs. For example:

Informed modern men and women do not consider adultery intrinsically wicked and sinful and therefore often commit it with little or no guilt or anxiety.

They are well able, with use of modern contraceptive techniques, to avoid the dangers of unwed pregnancy and abortion; and with the use of prophylactic measures and the selection of appropriate partners, they can avoid venereal infection.

They often need not worry about loss of reputation, since in modern society they may gain rather than lose reputation by engaging in extramarital affairs.

They need not commit adultery under sordid conditions, or on a non-loving basis, as they frequently can arrange to have loving and rewarding affairs.

They need not jeopardize their marriages, because adulterous affairs which are not known to one's mate can actually help enhance and preserve one's marriage rather than destroy it.

In view of these facts of modern life, it is doubtful whether many of the old arguments against adultery still hold too much water. At the same time, several of the advantages of premarital sex, which we examined in the previous chapter, also hold true for adultery.

Thus, literally millions of men and women who engage in adulterous affairs thereby gain considerable adventure and experience, become more competent at sexual pursuits and practices, are enabled to engage in a wide variety of sex acts, and have substantial amounts of sexual and nonsexual fun that they otherwise would be denied. These, in a world that tends to be dull and drab for average people, are no small advantages.

Should, then, the informed and healthy husbands and wives in our society blithely go about committing adultery? The answer, paradoxically enough, seems to be, in most cases, no. This is so for several reasons.

First, although, in some ideal society, it is quite probable that husbands and wives could be adulterous with impunity, and might well gain more than they lose thereby, ours is definitely not such an ideal society. For better or worse, we raise individuals to *feel* that their marriages are in jeopardy and that they are unloved if their mates have extramarital affairs.

Whether, under these circumstances, adultery actually *does* destroy marriages or *does* prove lack of love, is beside the point. Once one is raised to *feel* that these things are true, they tend to *become* true; and, under adulterous circumstances, damage often *is* therefore done to marriage. It might be much better if spouses convinced themselves that they *could* continue to love each other and live amicably together while still, at least occasionally, permitting themselves above-board extramarital affairs. But when they do not adopt this kind of sensible attitude toward adultery, they often endanger their marriages by engaging in it.

Thus, because people in our culture *believe* adultery wrecks marriage, husbands and wives who engage in it generally have to do so secretly and furtively. This means that they must be dishonest with their mates; and, although their adultery in itself might not harm their marriages, their *dishonesty* about their adultery (as about any other major issue) may prove to be harmful.

Similarly, because, in our society, married couples are supposed to achieve sex satisfaction only with each other, if one mate is an adulterer he will often tend to have less sex interest in the other mate than he normally would have; and, in consequence, may very well become sexually deprived and maritally discontent.

By the same token, since many individuals in our society have limited financial resources, time, and energy, an adulterous mate by devoting efforts to his (or her) inamorata may well deprive his mate in these non-sexual respects.

If people have a good all-around marriage, and if their mates might well be quite unhappy and might possibly divorce them if they were discovered to have an adulterous affair, they would then be jeopardizing their marriage for additional satisfactions which might hardly be worth the risk.

If this is so, individuals who have good marriages may be foolish to risk separating largely for the opportunity to have adulterous sex pleasures—which may often be their main gain from affairs. On the other hand, individuals with poor marriages take little risks, and often might just as well risk adulterous affairs.

In general, the risks you take in committing adultery behind your mate's back are the same risks you take in making any major dishonest move. Thus, if you invest the family savings in a new Cadillac, or decide to discontinue the use of contraceptives without informing your mate, you are being maritally uncooperative, and risk your partner's severe displeasure.

By the same token, if you are secretly adulterous, you are hardly cooperative with your mate, and risk her or his discovering this fact and their being highly displeased (not to mention hysterical) about your affair. Quite aside, then, from the sexual aspects of adultery, which are highly emphasized in American society, the secret commission of any major act with which your mate is concerned is likely to adversely affect your relationship with this mate.

This, then, would seem to be the major issue here: not adultery itself and its so-called moral consequences, but the consequences of being dishonest with one's mate, and through this dishonesty risking your impeding mutual trust, confidence, and working on your partnership.

In view of these facts, it is questionable whether well-adjusted, educated individuals in our society should normally commit furtive adultery—at least, if they want to perpetuate a presumably good marriage. If they are not themselves married (but are committing adultery with sex relations with someone who is), or if they are already unhappily married, then they may have little to lose by engaging in extramarital affairs.

If they are married happily and they and their mate honestly and mutually believe that adultery is a good thing, and are not at all disturbed by the knowledge of each other's infidelities, then again they may have nothing to lose. But the chances of their and their mate's having such a liberal attitude toward adultery if they were both raised in our culture are slim.

Otherwise stated, it does not appear to be very difficult for undisturbed and informed men and women in our civilization to accept fully the fact that premarital sex relations are a good thing and to become quite guilt-free in this connection. But, as yet, it does appear to be difficult for them to accept the fact that they and their mates may be adulterous without sabotaging their marriages. Several past and present societies other than our own have condoned adultery; and it is possible that we, too, may do so sometime in the future. For the present, however, adultery, except under certain limited circumstances (such as an individual's being away from home for a long time), would appear to be impractical rather than sinful for most people.

Today's adulterers need not feel evil or wicked. But, from the standpoint of impairing their own marriage, they may well be acting irrationally or neurotically. If they think of adultery not in terms of sin but in terms of the possible *adulteration* of their own marital happiness, they should be able to make wiser choices in this connection.

After publishing the foregoing remarks in *The Independent*, I received a remarkable letter from a middle-aged psychologist which raises some interesting questions in relation to adultery. My psychological correspondent, whom I shall call Dr. X, states that he married a childhood sweetheart when he was 25, had a so-so marriage with her, managed to have satisfactory sex relations, and was a faithful, most respectable husband and father (of five children) for 22 years. Finally, in his late forties, he had his first extramarital affair with "a handsome and attractive woman with a divine bell-like voice."

About this affair, Dr. X writes: "For the first time I was in love, and even more, for the first time I learned what passion could be. Very early I became sure it could not last—I was scared of my own inadequacy to keep pace with my lover's passion and with her genuine acceptance of what could be called free love.

"I was still pretty fiercely monogamous, though to my surprise I found no difficulty in having sexual relations with my lover and two days later, with my wife at home. My family obligations also kept me from even considering a divorce at this time."

Dr. X insists that this relationship "did tremendous things for me" and even made his marriage better for a while.

A year later, after the first affair had ended, he had a love affair with the widow of a cherished friend while he was away from home for six months. He says that "nothing in the whole affair is remembered with regret—just steady, warm satisfaction. There was sorrow but no hurt in the parting. And as before, the effect on my marriage was to make me for a time more affectionate, more understanding of my wife, better able to put up with the difficulties of our basic incompatibility."

Dr. X then had an unsatisfactory affair with a woman

much younger than he; and notes that "this relation did *not* help my marriage. Curious, isn't it? That when I find satisfaction elsewhere, my relation to my wife improves; when I fail elsewhere, it does not."

When his youngest child finished school, Dr. X divorced his wife and later married a woman with whom he had for some time been having an adulterous affair. Both this woman and her former husband had been having, by mutual agreement, extramarital affairs since the first year of their marriage. As long as they felt that their own marriage was solid they did not mind each other's infidelities.

On one occasion, the second Mrs. X and her first husband swapped partners with a couple with whom they were friendly, and all four lived amicably together under the same roof for several months. Finally, however, Mrs. X's first husband permanently took up with still another woman; and Dr. X's adulterous affair with her began, and later led to their marrying.

At this time, Dr. X reports, "I was still a bit more inclined to the monogamous point of view. She insisted that a nonrestricting attitude was a necessity for love, that one could not fully love while denying what might be a rewarding experience for the partner. I know that I grew in my understanding not of sex but of love, as we worked our way through this problem. I'd have given anything to have got some of these insights before my earlier marriage.

"But I still wasn't sure. So one day, learning that my wife's first love, Carl, was passing through our city, suggested that she invite him to stop over for a visit. I deliberately courted the trial. Could I take it if she were to renew her old and sweet intimacy?

"I slept with her the night before Carl was to make an early arrival; then, before dawn, went away to give him a clear field. And I did find it in me to say to myself and deeply to feel: 'I want my darling to be happy with Carl whatever form that happiness takes.' I think I really wanted them to have sex intimacy. At any rate, I went home full of a kind of pride in myself and a joyful loving peace. That was a high point in my whole life.

"Later, I joined Carl and my beloved for breakfast, and we had a fine time till his train arrived. It would be good to be able to say that I don't know nor care whether they had been intimate. I didn't ask but was told: she felt that our own relation was still too absorbing and rejected Carl's gentle inquiry. So in perfect honesty I said, 'Perhaps later you may feel otherwise. You know that if you do, I shall not be concerned.' Nor shall I."

Later, with another old lover of his wife's Dr. X's newly gained attitude was actually tested. Mrs. X comforted and slept with this old lover and told Dr. X what she had done. He notes: "I can say quite certainly that I was *glad* for her, and felt no loss of anything."

Dr. X concludes his letter with these observations: "Love is not a quantum that is lessened when divided. It is a growing system that increases with activity, like a living organism. True, it is subject, to use Gardner Murphy's term, to some degree of canalization. Constant adultering might divert love away from one person.

"In any kind of social arrangement there are grave problems regarding the management of love and sex. In our own society, adultery no doubt takes more intelligent thoughtfulness than is usually available. But I think we ought to keep in mind the *values* of multiple sex and love relations. Not just sex satisfaction alone, but love.

"That makes adultery dangerous. But it can mean great personal growth. I could not possibly love my wife as I do if it had not been for my adulterous love affairs. And she would not have been my beloved if she had not been able to open her love as she did to several men."

Dr. X's letter—the whole of which is ten pages long and has other pertinent things to say besides those quoted here—is most sincere and persuasive. In considering stories like his, and many more I have heard which are similar, I am compelled, once again, to be skeptical of all sweeping generalizations about human conduct.

Granted that a tabooed and legally penalized mode of behavior, such as adultery, has its distinct disadvantages; it must also be admitted that it has real advantages.

Granted that it is silly, childish, and self-defeating under one set of circumstances, it can also be inordinately valuable and ennobling under other circumstances.

Granted that certain individuals in our anti-adulterous communities could never tolerate their own or their partner's extramarital affairs, it is clear that certain other individuals—such as Dr. and Mrs. X—cannot only stoically bear, but actually find genuine satisfaction, in their own cuckoldry.

If we wish to be psychologically smug here, we may insist that people like Dr. and Mrs. X, who are originally raised with the prevalent puritanical notions of our society, cannot possibly *really* accept their own or their spouses' adulterous affairs. We may say that, unconsciously if not consciously, their liberal and permissive attitudes toward sex are underlain by more resentful and guilty attitudes, and that therefore they cannot receive *genuine* happiness from accepting or engaging in adultery.

This kind of psychodynamic analysis, however, is unscientific, since it gets you going and coming. If you say that you like white, it insists that you really unconsciously

41

prefer black but are afraid to admit this. And if you say that you like black, it says that you really, unconsciously prefer white. It leaves this kind of "thinking," with no room for *conscious* preferences.

Moreover, it is unconstructive and defeatist in that it denies all possibilities of basic human change. Admitting that people, once they have learned that white is good and black is bad, *have difficulty* in convincing themselves otherwise, that is not to say that they find changing their convictions *impossible*. If this were true, virtually no human progress would ever occur.

It is my firm conviction, therefore, that Dr. X did, in spite of his original puritanical upbringing, significantly change his attitudes toward adultery, and that he *was* able to not merely resentfully tolerate but actually enjoy some of his wife's infidelities. And not, I would be willing to wager, because he was masochistic, repressive, of perverse—but because he was now more civilized, humane, and loving.

So much for Dr. X. The rest of us are actually the heart of the matter. Are *we* able to be happier, emotionally healthier, and more loving by being adulterous? In the main, considering what our prejudicial upbringing has been, I am afraid not. But even this is not the full answer.

The full answer, I think, is: Some of us are able to benefit from adultery and some of us are not. Do we dare, then, make an invariant rule for *all* of us?

Aside from its potential disadvantages, which I think I have covered in this chapter, adultery has its definite advantages for many individuals in our society and even for society itself. Let me briefly list a number of them:

1. Normal people, as history has shown, are both biologically and socially, as Steve Salerno succinctly points out, "programmed to stray." This is especially true for

men; and Arnold Buss and a host of evolutionary psychologists have pointed out that their adulterous and varietist tendencies have often helped human procreation and the preservation of the race.

2. The steady maintenance of prostitution and semi-prostitution (e.g., sex massage) throughout the world, and its legalization in many cities (such as Reno and Amsterdam) has proven that millions of males can hardly be kept from patronizing prostitutes and, in spite of its risks and drawbacks, will continue doing so. Note: A high percentage of prostitute's patrons are married men.

3. Sex swinging, mate-swapping, and threesomes, which often involve married couples, are reasonably popular in America, frequently among politically conservative couples. No matter how difficult they are to arrange and keep going, a surprisingly large number of married (and single) people keep engaging in this kind of adultery. Even with the threat of AIDS very much around, surveys suggest that 2 to 4 percent practice swinging today.

4. Polygamy, the marriage of one man to two or more women, is practiced in some parts of the Sahara desert, in several Muslim nations, and although it has been banned since 1840 by the Mormons, a number of Mormon groups still continue to practice it. In spite of its economic hazards—a polygamous husband has to *support* two or more wives—polygamy still flourishes.

5. David P. Barash is a psychologist with a Ph.D. in zoology and his wife, Judith Eve Lipton, M.D., is a psychiatrist. They have written a remarkably well researched book, *The Myth of Monogamy*, that shows how for many

centuries infidelity has been very common in animals and people. Thus, unmarried U.S. college student men wanted as many as 18 different sex partners during their lifetime, while women wanted 4 to 5 sex partners.

Barash and Lipton, after making their study, say that it seems undeniable that humans are "mildly polygynous creatures whose 'natural' system probably involved one man mated, when possible, to more than one woman." A cross-cultural review of 56 different societies found that infidelity rates show that females and males "are remarkably similar." As Barash and Lipton summarize, it takes two to do the adultery tango. "And human beings love to dance."

6. Barash and Lipton also quote Bertrand Russell in *Marriage and Morals* as saying that the Christian view that adultery is immoral was based on the view that all intercourse, even in marriage, was "bad." A view of this sort, said Russell, "which goes against the biological facts can hardly be regarded by sane people as a morbid aberration." No wonder that there are so many adulterers who do *not* follow it!

7. Adultery has many of the same advantages as premarital sex. By engaging in it, particularly with the consent of their marital partners, people learn more about their own sex inclinations and those of their partners; they become less inhibited; they sometimes conquer their own feelings of sex inadequacy and gain more sex competency; they may learn practices from their adulterous partners that they may bring back to their marital partners.

Ira Reiss, who is now professor emeritus of sociology at the University of Minnesota, has been a pioneer in researching premarital and adulterous relationships in America ever since his book, *The Social Context of Premarital Permissiveness*, appeared in 1967. After considerable study of these sexual behaviors, he recently once again concluded that the new ethic in many western world countries accepts the widespread existence and the advantages of nonmarital sex. He calls the new ethic of sexual pluralism, "HER". The HER ethic calls for *Honesty, Equality,* and *Responsibility* in premarital and adulterous relationships—rather than the old ethic which we might call DII: *Dishonesty, Inequality,* and *Irresponsibility.*

Actually, as a large number of recent biographies have shown, a very many outstanding and accomplished men and women have largely followed what Reiss calls the philosophy of HER even when they were raised in conventional, antipluralistic sex cultures. I recently read over a sample of recent biographies of famous people that I have collected and that I may someday write about. Almost all of the biographers show that these celebrities had a number of premarital and/or adulterous affairs during their lifetime—and that quite a few of them were amazingly promiscuous considering the notable literary, artistic, musical, political, scientific, philosophic, and other works they produced.

Here, in alphabetical order, is a quick sampling of twentieth and twenty-first century celebrities I found to be decidedly unconventional in their sex lives: A.J. Ayer, Maria Callas, Bill Clinton, Hart Crane, Max Eastman, Albert Einstein, Rudy Giuliani, Graham Greene, Dashiel Hammett, Vaclav Havel, John F. Kennedy, Alfred Kinsey, Arthur Koestler, Norman Mailer, Edna St. Vincent Millay, George Moore, Iris Murdoch, Aristotle Onassis, Richard Rodgers, Arturo Toscanini, Frank Wedeking, H.G. Wells,

Rebecca West, The Duke and Duchess of Windsor, and Mao Zedong.

Quite a coterie of sex practitioners—of whom I have named just a few. This proves, pretty clearly, I think, that when men and women achieve high positions in life they very frequently feel that, even when sex is restricted in their culture, they can get away with engaging in premarital and adulterous affairs. And a hell of a lot of them, despite the obvious risks, do engage. History is full of non-monogamous sex-love pairings and will most likely continue to be. Even when they are severely banned and punished, their advantages and joys clearly prevail. Is there a good case for our minimally restricting them? I strongly suggest that there is.

5

The Justification of Sex
Without Love

A scientific colleague of mine, who holds a professorial post in the department of sociology and anthropology at one of our leading universities, asked me about my stand on the question of people having sexual relations without love. Although I have taken something of a position on this issue in my book, *The American Sexual Tragedy*, I have never quite considered the problem in sufficient detail. So here goes.

In general, I feel that affectional, as against nonaffectional, sex relations are *desirable* but not *necessary*. It is usually desirable that an association between coitus and affection exist—particularly in marriage, because it is often difficult for two individuals to keep finely tuned to each other over a period of years, and if there is not considerable love between them, one may tend to feel sexually imposed upon by the other.

The fact, however, that the coexistence of sex and love may be desirable does not, to my mind, make it necessary. In fact, many individuals—including, even, many married couples—*do* find greater satisfaction in having sex relations without than with love. I do not consider it fair to label

47

these individuals as "abnormal" just because they may be in the minority.

Moreover, even if they are in the minority (as may well *not* be the case), I am sure that they number literally millions of men and women. If so, they constitute a sizable subgroup of humans whose rights to sex satisfaction preferably should be fully acknowledged and protected.

Even if we consider the supposed majority of individuals who find greater satisfaction in sex-love than in sex-sans-love relations, it is doubtful if all or most of them do so for *all* their lives. During much of their existence, especially their younger years, these people tend to find sex-without-love quite satisfying, and sometimes even to prefer it to affectional sex.

When they become older, and their sex drives tend to wane, they may well emphasize coitus with rather than without affection. But why should we condemn them *while* they still prefer sex to sex-love affairs?

Many individuals, especially females in our culture, who say that they only enjoy sex when it is accompanied by affection, are usually unthinkingly conformist and perhaps unconsciously hypocritical. If they were able to contemplate themselves objectively, and had the courage of their inner convictions, they might also find sex without love eminently gratifying.

This is not to say that they would *only* enjoy non-affectional coitus, nor that they would always find it *more* satisfying than affectional sex. But, in the depths of their psyche and soma, they would deem sex without love pleasurable *too*.

And why should they not? And why should we, by puritanical attitudes, force these individuals to drive a considerable portion of their sex feelings and potential satisfaction underground?

If, in other words, we view sex-love relations as desirable rather than necessary, we sanction the innermost thoughts and drives of many of our fellow men and fellow women to have sex *and* sex-love relations. If we take the opposing view, we hardly destroy their innermost thoughts and drives, but frequently tend to intensify them while denying them open and honest outlet. As Freud pointed out, this is one (though by no means the only) instigator of neurosis.

Since sex is a biological, as well as a social, drive, and in its biological element, is essentially non-affectional, we can expect that, however we try to civilize the sex drives—and civilize them to *some* degree we had better—there will always be an underlying tendency for them to escape from our social shackles and to be still partly felt in the raw.

When so felt, when our biosocial sex urges lead us to desire and enjoy sex without (as well as with) love, I do not see why we should try to make their experiencers feel needlessly guilty and ashamed.

Many individuals—millions in our society, I fear—have little or no capacity for affection or love. Some of these individuals, perhaps, may be emotionally disturbed, and should preferably be helped to increase their affectional propensities. But a large number are not generally disturbed, and still have little capacity for loving.

Mentally deficient persons, for example, as well as many dull normals (who, together, include several million citizens of our nation) are notoriously shallow in their feelings, and probably intrinsically so. Since these individuals are for the most part *not* going to overcome their deficiencies, and since most of them definitely *do* have sex desires, I again see no point in making them guilty when they have nonloving sex. Surely these unfortunate individuals are sufficiently handicapped by their impairments without our adding to their woes by damning them when they manage to achieve some nonloving sexual release.

At times some people find more satisfaction in nonloving sex even though, under other circumstances, these *same* people may find more satisfaction in sex-love affairs. Thus, the man who *normally* enjoys being with his girl-friend because he loves as well as is sexually attracted to her, may occasionally find immense satisfaction in being with another woman who he definitely does not love.

Granting that this may be (or is it?) unusual, I do not see why it should be condemned.

If many people get along excellently and cooperatively with business partners, employees, professors, laboratory associates, acquaintances, and even spouses for whom they have little or no love or affection, but with whom they have certain specific things in common, I do not see why there cannot be individuals who get along excellently and most cooperatively with sex partners with whom they may have little else in common.

I personally can easily see the plight of a man who spends much time with a woman with whom he has nothing in common but sex. Since I believe that life is too short to be well consumed in relatively one-track or intellectually low-level pursuits, I would also think it rather unrewarding for a woman to spend much time with a man with whom she had mutually satisfying sex, friendships, and cultural interests but no love involvement. This is because I would like to see people, in their years of life, have maximum rather than minimum satisfactions with individuals of the other sex or the same sex with whom they spend considerable time.

I can easily see, however, even the most intelligent and

highly cultured individuals spending a *little* time with a sex partner with whom they have common sex and cultural but no real love interests. And I feel that, for the time expended in this manner, their lives may be definitely enriched.

Moreover, when I encounter friends or clients who become enamored and spend considerable time and effort thinking about and being with partners with whom they are largely sexually obsessed, and for whom they have little or no love, I mainly view their sexual infatuations as one of the results of their being human. For humans are the kind of animals who are easily disposed to this type of behavior.

I believe that one of the distinct inconveniences or tragedies of human sexuality is that it endows us, and perhaps particularly the males among us, with a propensity to become exceptionally involved and infatuated with members of the other (or same) sex whom, had we no sex urges, we would hardly notice. That is too bad; and it might well be a better world if it were otherwise. But it is *not* otherwise, and I think it is silly for us to condemn ourselves because we are that way in this respect.

We had better *accept* our biosocial tendencies instead of constantly blaming ourselves and futilely trying to change certain of our harmless, though perhaps disadvantageous, characteristics.

For reasons such as these, I feel that although it is usually—if not always—*desirable* for human beings to have sex relations with those they love rather than with those they do not love, it is by no means *necessary* that they do so. When we teach them that it *is* necessary, we only needlessly encourage millions of our citizens to feel guilt, shame, and self-damnation.

The position that I take—that there are several good reasons why affectional, as against non-affectional, sex relations are desirable but not necessary—can be assailed on several counts. I shall now consider some of the objections to this position to see if I can answer them.

It may be claimed that people who have non-loving instead of loving sex relations are not necessarily wicked but that they are self-defeating because, while going for immediate gratification, they miss out on even greater enjoyments. But this would only be true if such individuals (whom we shall assume, for the sake of discussion, *would* get greater enjoyment from affectional sex relations than from non-affectional ones) *usually* or *always* have non-affectional coitus. If they were *occasionally* or *sometimes* having love with sex, and the rest of the time having sex without love, they would be missing very little, if any, enjoyment.

Under these circumstances, in fact, they would get *more* pleasure from *sometimes* having sex without love. For the fact remains that in our present-day society sex without love is often *more frequently* available than sex with love. For example, millions of married couples dislike and even hate each other and yet often manage to have quite enjoyable sex. Surprising?

Consequently, to ignore non-affectional coitus when affectional coitus is not available would be sheer folly. In regard both to immediate *and* greater enjoyment, many people would thereby lose out.

The claim can be made, of course, that if people sacrifice sex without love *now*, they will experience more pleasure by having sex with love in the future. This is an interesting claim; but I find no empirical evidence to sustain it. It is akin to the belief that if people starve themselves for several days in a row they will greatly enjoy eating a meal at the end of a week or a month. I am sure some will—provided that they are not too sick or debilitated to enjoy anything! But, even assuming that such people derive enormous satisfaction from this one meal a week or a month, is their *total* satisfaction greater than it would have been had they enjoyed three good meals a day for that same time period? I doubt it.

So with sex. People who starve themselves sexually for a long period of time—as virtually everyone who rigidly sticks to the sex with love doctrine must—will (perhaps) *ultimately* achieve greater satisfaction when they do find sex with love than they would have experienced had they been sexually freer. But, assuming that this is so, will their *total* satisfaction be greater?

It may be claimed that if both sex with and without love are encouraged in any society, non-affectional sex will drive out affectional sex, somewhat in accordance with Gresham's laws of currency. On the contrary, however, there is much reason to believe that just because people have sex, for quite a period, on a non-affectional basis, they will be more than eager to replace it, eventually, with sex with love.

From my clinical experience, I have often found that men who most want to settle down with a single mistress or wife are those who have tried several lighter affairs and found them wanting. The view that sex without love eradicates the need for affectional sex relationships is somewhat akin to the ignorance is bliss theory. For it says that if people never experienced sex with love they would never realize how good it was and therefore would never strive for it.

The proponents of this theory seem to be saying that sex without love is so greatly satisfying, and sex with love so difficult and disadvantageous, that given the choice between the two, most people would pick the former. If this is so, then by all means let them pick the former—with which, in terms of their greater and total happiness, they would presumably be better off.

I doubt, however, that this hypothesis is factually sustainable. From clinical experience, again, I can say that individuals who are capable of sex with love usually seek and find it, while those who remain non-affectional in their sex affairs often are not particularly capable of sex with love and may require psychotherapeutic help before they can become thus capable.

As a therapist, I frequently work with individuals who are only able to achieve non-affectional sex affairs, and although helping them eliminate their irrational fears makes it possible for them to achieve sex-love relationships, I still would doubt that *all* persons who take no great pleasure in sex with love are emotionally deficient. Some quite effective individuals—such as Immanuel Kant, for instance—seem to be so wholeheartedly dedicated to *things* or *ideas* that they rarely or never become amatively involved with people.

As long as such individuals have vital, creative interests and are intensely absorbed or involved with *something*, I would hesitate to diagnose them as being necessarily neurotic merely because they do not ordinarily become intensely involved with *people. Some* of these nonloving but sexually enjoying people are neurotic. But *all* of them? Hardly!

Neurotic or not, I see no reason why people who are dedicated to things or ideas should not have, in most instances, normal sex urges. If they do, I fail to see why they should not consummate their sexuality in nonloving ways and perhaps have more time and energy for the things and ideas to which they are dedicated.

It may be objected that people's sex urges are not merely biological, but *biosocial*; and that some restrictions, such as the banning of non-affectional sex relations, have to be put on them in order to make for the common good. This, to some extent, is true. People, in fact, must inhibit their sex interests in certain respects if they are to live with others in a cooperative, undestructive way.

The question is, should people's self-imposed social-sexual restrictions be minimal or maximal?

Certainly, humans had better not rape others; nor pretend that they love to win sex favors; nor take sexual advantage of minors. But, assuming that two adults, who are honest with each other, *want* to have non-loving sex relations for a day, a year, or forever—what is uncooperative, anti-social, or harmful about *that*?

Socially, there is little doubt that most men and women *can* be raised so that they come to strongly desire sex only when it is accompanied by love so that they make themselves guilty about their non-affectional sex affairs. They *can* be reared to do this. But why *should* they be?

In fact, I take an opposing view: namely, that sex with instead of without love *may* for *some* people be *preferable* rather than *necessary*; and that forcing a sex-love philosophy and activity on *all* people will most probably lead to *less* human happiness and help contribute to *more* emotional disturbance.

It may be alleged that if people have non-affectional sex their activity will be alienated from and unacceptable to the rest of their personality, and that therefore they will develop severe internal conflicts. The answer to this is that such conflicts do not exist innately but are almost entirely aided by puritanical sex teachings—such as the teaching that sex without love is pointless or wicked.

Without this kind of sex teaching, some individuals might have mild conflicts between sexually enjoying themselves in a non-affectional manner or waiting until a full-blown love affair between them and a suitable partner ensued. But if we did not deliberately teach people that sex without love is unjustified and worthless, I'll bet that most of their conflicts concerning this kind of behavior would vanish!

It may be contended that if love without sex were not discouraged or proscribed, an increase in adultery would occur. Assuming that such an increase would be undesirable, I would present a reverse hypothesis: namely that the greater the emphasis we place on the idea that sex must only be had with love, the greater tendency there will be for men and women to commit adultery.

This is because in many American marriages, for reasons which I need not go into at the moment, little love seems to remain between the partners after the first few years. But sex relations, for the most part, continue. If these sex relations without love were to stop, as the proponents of the sex-must-be-had-with-love theory advocate, then literally millions of husbands and wives who have been married for, say, ten or more years would take to adultery—where it is probable that many would find, at least for a while, sex with love.

The notion that sex must be accompanied by love is a rather romantic notion that does not square well with modern sociological concepts of marriage, since most of the experts in the field note that marriage, in order to be lastingly happy, should be somewhat de-romanticized. Both romantic love and sex satisfaction, I would say, are most easily maintained if people who seek them change their partners frequently. Consequently, if one *insists* that love and sex must go together, one thereby virtually dooms the continuation of millions of marriages that now, albeit none too ecstatically, are maintained.

It is sometimes held that since the value of sex without affection is exceptionally small compared to the value of sex with affection, the former should be discouraged in favor of the latter. This is an exceptionally weak argument because, in my estimation (as well, apparently, as that of literally millions of other humans), sex without affection has a very strong, positive value in, of, by, and for itself. The fact that sex with affection may have a still stronger, more positive value for some or most individuals should not be used to denigrate the value of sex without love.

I personally feel that a fine chunk of roast pork or fillet is distinctly more nutritious and satisfying than a box of candy, but I would hardly try to turn people against eating sweets. If people like candy more than steak, that is their value, and although I disagree with it, I respect it as a value different from my own.

Similarly, if millions of people think that sex without love is as good as or better than sex with love, I again disagree with but respect their evaluation. Maybe they would be better off if they gave up loveless sex for sex with affection; but I, for one, am not going to try to force them to do so.

It may be objected that it is the responsibility of social thinkers and public officials to raise the standards of the populace for the greater good and enjoyment of this populace; and that therefore sex with affection should be highly touted while affectionless sexuality should be scorned and banned. To this objection to sex without love I would offer several rebuttals:

1. Granting—for the sake of discussion—that people might be better off if they raised their standards of sexual participation, the question is: Should they be *forced* to do so?

   Many Americans would doubtlessly be happier and better occupied if they listened to classical music and viewed Shakespearean plays on TV rather than if they listened to popular music and viewed quiz shows. But does this mean that we should jail the rock-and-roll addicts or try to make the quiz show viewers feel thoroughly ashamed of themselves?

   A psychological colleague asked me what was my attitude toward forced conciliation when people came to court for marital difficulties. I replied that (a) I definitely thought, on the basis of my experience, that individuals who are forced into psychotherapy or counseling can often, even though it is at first against their will, learn to benefit from this counseling and thus save their marriages; but that (b) I would not, under any circumstances, want to have them *forced*, either by direct coercion or encouraging them to be terribly guilty, into resorting to conciliation. I am more—perhaps idealistically—attached to the notion of the value of human individuality and freedom than I am to the notion of forcing people to be "better off."

   I am also reminded, in this connection, of a talk by an authority on criminology, who pointed out that dictatorships invariably have less gangsterism and criminality than we have in our kind of democracy. The question he raised was: Is the social cost of such "benefits" too high? I think it is.

   Even, then, were I firmly convinced that humans would be better off if they refrained from loveless sex affairs and only confined themselves to loving ones, I would balk at coercing them into following my belief. The "cure" in this instance would, I am afraid, be worse than the "disease."

2. Assuming that it might be better if men and women refrained from sex without affection, the fact is that such a general change in human behavior is not going to take place for at least decades to come. In the meantime, whether we like it or not, we are going to continue to live in a world where countless individuals *do* have and enjoy loveless sex affairs. If this is so, why should we help create needless guilt and despair among the residents of our *existing* society by scorning or penalizing them for having sex without love?

3. Although I personally prefer classical to popular music and Hamlet to quiz shows, I would hate to see a world in which there was *no* popular music or quiz programs. Even highly intelligent, educated, and cultured individuals, I am sure, will *sometimes* want to listen to or view "cheap" entertainment. Similarly, even people who *largely* enjoy sex with affection will, I think, *sometimes* thoroughly, even ecstatically, enjoy sex without affection. And why should they not?

It is often concluded that, because America is a basically puritanical country, it will never accept sex without affection; and that therefore, rather than condemn young people to abstinence before marriage, we should encourage them to accept sex with affection—which, presumably, the nation as a whole will tolerate. This, it seems to me, is a rather defeatist position. The fact is that where many highly respectable Americans now are able to accept sex with but not without love, a century ago the same kind of

Americans were only able to accept sex with marriage and viewed all non-marital relations, however lovingly based, as despicable and worthless.

If, in the course of the last century, such a drastic change has taken place in our sex mores that affectional non-marital relations are now being accepted where they previously were thoroughly condemned, there is reason to believe that in the course of the next half century non-affectional non-marital relations may also become equally acceptable.

The argument that because something is not now socially approved, and that therefore people who engage in this disapproved act will get into difficulties and would be more sensible to refrain, is tautological. Of course people who perform socially unsanctioned actions will find themselves criticized and, sometimes, penalized. The question we are discussing, however, is not whether those who have sex without love in present-day America will be socially disapproved; but *should* they be?

As noted above, the fact seems to be that from an *individual* viewpoint, loveless sex affairs seem to be exceptionally fine for many men and women—otherwise, it is difficult to see why they go to such great lengths to have them. From a *social* viewpoint, however, the fact is also clear that our customs and mores often condemn such unaffectional affairs. The question therefore arises: Are the social, and much flouted, rules sane and sensible?

The liberal proponents of the sex-should-be-had-only-with-love theory hold that the social banning of loveless sex is sensible because (a) sex is far better with than without love and (b) people should be encouraged or forced to see this.

In regard to point (a), conservatives may have a reasonable argument—if only they would modify it to read:

Sex is far better with than without love for *some* individuals under *some* conditions. In regard to point (b), they have a far less cogent argument. For even assuming that affectional affairs are usually preferable to non-affectional ones, it is still questionable whether those who benightedly fail to see this should be coerced into seeing the light by emotional blackmail, guilt-producing exhortations, and threats of severe social or legal penalties.

If the goodness of sex with love (or any other mode of human behavior) cannot be effectively encouraged without this kind of verbal and statutory bludgeoning, it is to be seriously wondered just how "good" it really is in the first place and how "beneficial" the tactics of its adherents are in the second place.

Rather than go along with the well-meaning but questionable views of the upholders of the sex-must-be-wedded-to-love theory, I would much prefer to take my stand with Voltaire. Although I may not personally favor sex without love to affectional sex affairs, I shall fight for the rights of those who do.

Just for the record: Are there any special *advantages* of your—or my, or anyone's—having sex without love instead of with love? Obviously there are for some of the people some of the time—and, most probably, for some of the people all of the time.

One clear advantage stems from the fact that loving your partner and even being loved by one or more partners clearly takes time and energy—just as loving gardening, or a sport, or novel writing does. Practically all of us have, during our *one* life, limited time and effort. Maybe, if we dwell in hell or heaven, we'll have more time. Maybe! But in this one life we *do* have, we may like love, even enjoy it intensely, but to also at times *choose* to delight—yes, delight—in loveless sex. As humans, we do have personal choices. Loveless sex may, for some of us some of the time, be one of them. And a pretty good one!

Also, loveless sex is often *more available* than sex embedded—not to mention *bedded*—with love. If so, why not enjoy it until the "real thing" comes along? While waiting for a luscious dessert at the end of a great meal, why not enjoy a little salad? Why not?

The fact that most of us may thrill to loving sex *far more* than to loveless sex hardly means that the latter kind is *no* good or *little* good. It can readily have its own delightful taste!

Consequently, the relatively *inferior* pleasure of sex without love to sex with love may enhance the delights of the latter when it does—alas, rarely!—come our way. Our having the common variety of sex may prime us for having—*when* we have it—the uncommon variety.

All kinds of sex—without as well as with love—can be learning *experiences* that increase the savor of *many* aspects of our lives, sexual and nonsexual. To live is to learn; and to learn is very often to live *more*.

If we have a steady diet of only sex with love and no sex without it, we may—as humans are wont to do—suffer from some degree of monotony, just as our steadily thrilling to classical music *or* to jazz or to rock and roll may become monotonous. Why not relieve our monotony by at times including some sex without love in our diet?

Let me conclude this chapter by saying again that I personally enjoy loving sex distinctly more than nonloving sex most (not all) of the time! But even if I *always* enjoyed it more, why should I insist on restricting *you* —and you and you—to *my* favorite cup of tea? For no good reason that I can see!

62

6

Why Americans Are So Fearful of Sex

In the whole wide world there may be no large group of people who are so fearful of sex as are we Americans.

The southern Europeans, such as the French and the Italians, are notoriously freer about many of their sex ways than we are. The northern Europeans, especially in Denmark and Holland, are often so enlightened about sex that they easily tolerate prostitution, nonmarital pregnancy, and gay relationships. The North Africans tend to live in what we would consider a hotbed of sexual vice.

Most Central African and Southern African natives have many customs, including polygamy, which we would look upon with horror. Asian and Middle East sex beliefs and practices are so much freer than ours in many ways that our modern sex manuals are just beginning to recently catch up with some of the knowledge which for centuries has been recorded in Persian, Hindu, and Chinese texts.

Even the English, from whom our Anglo-Saxon codes of sex conduct primarily stem, are in many ways less fearful of sex than we are. English newspapers and magazines publish details of sex crimes and happenings which would not be allowed in American publications. English sex manuals are not only more outspoken than American sex books but have a proportionately wider sale. The premarital and extramarital behavior of many English women is in many respects significantly less inhibited than that of our own women.

We Americans have a deceptively free exterior attitude about sex; but underneath we are chicken. We pet, as the Kinsey report shows, almost universally. We engage, to a considerable degree, in masturbatory, fornicative, adulterous, homosexual, and other types of sex outlets. But we often do so queasily, stealthily, guiltily. We cannot help our actions, as it were, but we can help our thoughts—and we do help them drive us to anxiety, despair, neurosis. We have our sexual cake, but we don't really eat it—or we gulp it down in such a manner as to bring on acute indigestion.

The result is considerable coolness by many of our women, varying degrees of impotence by males, and enormous amounts of dissatisfaction, unappeased hunger, and continual sex fear on the part of both.

Why?

Why should I and other psychotherapists spend so much time seeing a continuous succession of disturbed people, many of whom have some serious degree of sexual anxiety?

There are several important answers to these whys:

Americans are specifically taught to be fearful of sex

During their childhood and adolescence, all the possible dangers, and virtually none of the pleasures, of human sexuality are drummed into their heads and hearts. Grim specters of loss of reputation, "illegitimate" pregnancy, abortion, sexually transmitted diseases, "perversion," and physical and emotional breakdown are ceaselessly thrown at our young people.

The idea that sex is good, sex is fun, and sex is one of the greatest and most repeatable of human joys is rarely unequivocally brought to youngsters' attention. In jokes, yes; in sly asides, of course; in under-the-counter pamphlets and books, certainly. In these indirect and back-handed ways the idea that sex is good, hot, and spicy is slammed across to the average Americans. But directly and forthrightly? Heavens, no! Responsible sources come up with cavilings, quibblings, and cautionings instead.

The result, as I noted in *The Folklore of Sex*, is that the American boy and girl, and later the American man and woman, believe that sex is good—*and* bad; tasty—*and* nasty. They are, in a word, conflicted. And conflict means indecision and doubt—which means fear.

Americans are raised to be overly-competitive about sex

Our boys and girls are made to feel that, above all else, they must succeed, achieve, win out in the social-sexual game. They must not merely enjoy themselves on their dates and eventually achieve good marriages—nay, they must date the *best* boy or girl in the neighborhood; be the *finest* lover for miles around; have the *greatest* home and family.

Americans must do all these things, moreover, with little experience to speak of, without any notable period of learning. If they study arithmetic, French, or engineering, they are of course expected to take a while to get onto the subject, to learn it. But if they study what is one of the most complicated subjects in the world—namely, that of getting along well with a member of the other sex—they are somehow supposed to be able to discover all the answers with no learning experience and to make the best possible impression from scratch. This, of course, they usually cannot do. They naturally make a certain amount of blunders, errors, mistakes. But each error is considered to be an unforgivable crime. Each time when he misses her mouth and kisses her nose, or she goes a little too far or not far enough in petting, or either of them fails to say the right romantic word when the moon is full: each mistake is considered catastrophic, disastrous.

This means that our young people soon become afraid to try certain actions or chance certain words. Then, not acquiring any experience or familiarity with doing so, they become afraid of risking new experiences. Thus arises a vicious circle, where dire fear of making a social-sexual mistake leads to lack of learning, which in turn leads to further fear of ineptness, which in turn leads to further inhibition of learning, and so on to a hopeless eternity.

This also means that when young people who keep fruitlessly merry-go-rounding in this manner finally do stumble into marriage, they still have learned relatively little about social-sexual relations, and carry their fears and restraints into their marriages.

Americans are brought up to fear tenderness and love

American males, in particular, are raised to be "regular guys" and to avoid "sissified" displays of emotionality. They do not kiss, like the French; throw their arms around like the Italians; act very warm to their children, like many peoples of the world. Even American women are often raised so that they are ashamed to cry openly, to laugh uproariously, or to let their hair down in public.

This means that, in spite of our Hollywood films and romantic novels, we do not allow ourselves to be overly warm, affectionate, and loving. We often, in fact, try to use sex as a substitute for love: to throw ourselves into wild petting sessions because it is easier to say with our hands what we would be embarrassed to say with our lips.

But love inhibition breeds sex inhibition. As we inhibit and deaden our tender reactions, we also block some of our deepest sex sensations. Love, moreover, is an exceptionally good antidote for all kinds of fear; and to the extent that we have little love, we tend to have more fear—including sex fear.

Americans are often generally fearful and neurotic

We Americans tend to have unreasonable goals and ideals, especially in regard to worldly success and keeping up with the Joneses. We frequently are never weaned from our childhood ideas of grandiosity and refuse to face the harsh realities of life and accept the world as it is. We have seriously conflicting values and philosophies of life—such as the notion that we should be good and kind, on the one hand, and ruthlessly make a million dollars, on the other.

Because of our general insecurities, immaturities, and conflicts, we tend to have multitudinous feelings of doubt and inadequacy, which often lap over into our sexual attitudes. When general neurosis is epidemic, sexual disturbance is not likely to be too far away.

Innumerable specific examples can be found of American (as well as world-wide) puritanism, and its resulting in helping to make us, despite our recent increase in sexual liberalism, much more fearful of sex and guilty about various kinds of accepting it fully. Here are a few typical examples to twenty-first century of self- and society-defeating narrow-mindedness and censorship in sexual areas:

- As Steve Salerno indicates, although unsatisfying sex is a cause of frequent marital problems and great anxiety for millions of men and women, exceptionally little governmental and privately funded research is spent each year to discover more about enhancing erotic experiences.

• Some 43 percent of our women and 31 percent of our men when studied say that they have problems with sex. Again, although we spend some millions of dollars a year researching sexually transmitted diseases, we spend paltry sums researching sexual dissatisfaction problems.

• Although a huge study conducted by the Association for the Advancement of Retired Persons showed that while over 30 percent of men and women reported having sex difficulties, less than 13 percent of the men and less than 10 percent of the women had ever sought treatment for their problems. Most of the untreated people felt ashamed to even let a physician or a therapist know about their difficulties. Shame about talking to a health care professional about sex is so common that Dr. Charles Moser wrote a book, *Health Care Without Shame*.

• Many sex and marriage and family therapists find that a large number of the people who consult them are thoroughly guilty about having even the most innocent kinds of fantasies when they masturbate or have partner sex, especially when they fantasize having sex with another partner than the one they are with! But, as David Schnarch reports, "research says partner-replacement fantasies are the most common fantasies going." (!!!)

• Until recently, adulterous relationships among animals and humans were hidden even from biologists, zoologists, and other scientists.

• Betty Dodson, one of the most courageous and outspoken sex educators since 1970, has been censored by popular magazines and publishers from the start of her career up to the present day. Even the woman's liberation magazine, *Ms.*, refused to publish her "Liberating Masturbation." Betty reported in 2003 that her use of her own website on the Internet "was my first completely uncensored form of communication." I describe my own lifelong sex censorship problems in chapter 10 of this book.

• The Title V Abstinence Program of the U.S. Government offers grants to states for promoting absolute abstinence to young people and also teaches that the expected standard of human sexual activity for all Americans is to be found exclusively in faithfully kept monogamous marriage. The state of Alabama still has in effect its Anti-Obscenity Enforcement Act which prohibits the sale of "any device designed or marketed as useful primarily for the stimulation of human genital organs." The penalty? A maximum fine of $10,000 and up to one year of hard labor. In the year 2001, New York State, New Jersey, North Carolina, and several other states banned women public school students from wearing sexy dresses that included spaghetti straps, fishnet stockings and shirts, T-shirts with lewd messages, clothing more suited to the beach, and any clothing that "bares the private parts."

I could go on and on with surveys, therapists' and physicians' observations, and psychological and sociological writings that show an almost incredible number of instances where antisex prejudice *still* very much exists in the twenty-first century. But why continue? The above items and many more that I refer to in this book clearly show, as I said in the beginning of this chapter, that Americans (and many other people in today's world) are helped to be overly fearful, inhibited, prudish, phobic, and obsessive-compulsive about sex-love acts. Distinct progress in this respect has been made since I started conducting love, marital, and sex research in 1938, doing sex therapy in 1943, and writing on sex-love topics in 1945. I think I can safely say that one of the main influences on the American sex revolution in the 1960s was my own professional and public talks, workshops, and articles and books from 1945 onward. Alfred Kinsey and his collaborators in 1948 and 1953 and William Masters and Virginia Johnson in 1960 got more attention than I did for their liberal sex views. But, my many books, from 1951 onward especially, appreciably helped!

The moral of all this? Although sex in America (and the rest of the civilized world) began coming out of the closet in the 1940s and 1950s, and although sex suppression and guilt has been remarkably aided since that time, the closet door is still too tightly closed for my tastes. And, hopefully, for yours!

Assuming that Americans, because of reasons like the foregoing, may be the most sexually fearful of any other large group of people, the question arises: Can anything effective be done to make us less panicky in this respect? Certainly: but only if the problem is tackled in all its important ramifications, and not treated as if it were a simple sex problem alone.

On an individual basis, there are several things which you may do to overcome any irrational and destructive fears of sex that you may have.

First: Admit that you are sexually fearful, and do not try to hide your fear beneath a mask of false sophistication. You can honestly acknowledge that you have sex problems, instead of cavalierly attempting to dismiss them.

Second: You can obtain considerable factual information about sex, particularly in relation to your own fears. You can learn, from modern sex manuals and from talks with a physician or therapist, some of the facts about masturbation, sexual inadequacy, sex deviation, and other aspects of human sexuality which you may ignorantly fear.

Third: You can do some of the sex acts of which you are irrationally afraid. Experiment with coital or extracoital techniques which you "know" are normal and healthy, but which you still bigotedly believe are "bad" or "wicked."

Fourth: You can begin to consistently indoctrinate yourself *against* some of your senseless sex fears instead of continually reinforcing yourself with them. You can show yourself, over and over again, that acts like masturbation are *not* wrong, childish, or harmful. You can tell yourself that sex behavior that does not needlessly and definitely harm yourself and others is good, harmless, and beneficial, and should preferably be practiced as you want.

Fifth: If you try the foregoing techniques of helping yourself overcome your anxieties and you still have them, do not hesitate to go for psychological help. The chances are, in such a case, that they are neurotic and may be significantly alleviated by psychotherapy.

On a social basis, a concerted attack on the common sex fears that now inhabit and inhibit our population is certainly desirable at the present time and may be tried these ways:

1. Our society can end virtually all sex censorship. Such censorship certainly does not prevent the public from seeing the material that is publicly banned—indeed, it usually encourages the distribution of this material. It then makes banned sex materials more enticing *and*

"dangerous" than they would otherwise be.

2. We had better eliminate many of our antisexual laws. At most, as I noted in *The Psychology of Sex Offenders*, we preferably should only penalize those sex acts that involve the use of force or duress; or an adult's taking sexual advantage of a minor; or public sex acts which are distasteful to the majority of those in whose presence they are committed. Acts other than these, that are engaged in by consent between two competent adults, should not be subject to legal penalties.

3. We preferably should, as outlined in chapter 10 of this volume, give wholehearted attention to realistic and healthy sex education of our children, and should at all school and home levels, teach them to understand the facts of human sexuality.

4. We should establish sex institutes and clinics and train practitioners to whom sexually fearful individuals may go for suitable treatment.

5. We should particularly encourage and give financial backing for considerable research into important areas where irrational sex fear is now rampant.

If a concerted attack were made, along the foregoing individual and social lines, on the problem of sexual fear in our culture, it might not entirely disappear but would at least be reduced. Is the game, despite its difficulties, worth the candle? Or shall the defeatists among us, as they so often do, again win by default?

7

Adventures with Censorship

When I originally began writing the chapters of this book, Lyle Stuart wrote an editorial for *The Independent* about the difficulties I previously had trying to publish that material. Let me now recount some of my other first-hand adventures with sex censorship.

My serious encounters with sex censorship began when I contracted to write my first book, *The Folklore of Sex*. Charles Boni asked me to do this book for him; and, since he did not directly publish books himself, said that he would arrange to do so through one of the large publishers, as he had several times done before.

He accordingly submitted the outline of the book to Simon and Schuster, with whom he had excellent relations. He was told that they had got into some difficulty on a sex book they had published some twenty years previously, and that therefore it was their policy to touch no works in this field. Shortly thereafter, however, Simon and Schuster contracted to publish Abraham Franzblau's *The Road to Sexual Maturity*—surely one of the most reactionary books on sex.

Nothing daunted, Mr. Boni took the outline of *The*

Folklore of Sex to the world's largest publishers, Doubleday, who were quite enthusiastic about it and immediately contracted to publish the book. They were equally delighted with the manuscript and were so eager to send it to press that they arranged to do some of the retyping in their own offices.

Everything was set for publication in the fall of 1950 and galley and page proofs were speedily printed and corrected. The imprint on the title page was that of Doubleday & Company; and on the back of the title page was the usual statement found in all Doubleday books: "Printed in the United States at the Country Life Press, Garden City, N.Y."

Then something happened.

"Certain people" at Doubleday began to get quite distressed about the nature of the book when they were shown the page proofs. Their distress appeared to stem from the facts that the book took a (rather mildly) liberal attitude toward sex; that it quoted from many popular American newspapers and magazines whose editors might object to having their sexual proclivities exposed; and that it also ruthlessly revealed the frankly sexual underpinnings of numerous best-selling novels and non-fictional works, many of which were either published by Doubleday or distributed by one of the book clubs owned by them.

After several frantic conferences were held, publication of *The Folklore of Sex* was delayed; Doubleday's name was taken off the title page and Charles Boni's name substituted instead; publication was still further delayed; and the book finally appeared almost a half year after its originally planned publication date.

It was still printed at the Country Life Press and was distributed by Doubleday. But although editorial enthusiasm for it was sustained, and Mr. Boni did everything possible to aid its sale, promotional initiative at Doubleday noticeably dimmed.

Few reviews or publicity stories appeared in leading newspapers and magazines; The *New York Times* and the *Chicago Tribune* were not seriously opposed when they refused to publish any ads whatever on the book; and the volume was remaindered with unusual alacrity. Only when, a decade later, Grove Press published a revised edition of the book in paperback form, did it begin to attain real popularity.

So much for *The Folklore of Sex*.

My second book, *The American Sexual Tragedy*, was something of a sequel to the first book but Doubleday, who had an option to publish it, didn't even want to look at the manuscript. It was then accepted by Twayne Publishers, who had no vested interests in well-known authors or book clubs, and who were unusually liberal in their editing of the manuscript.

Where Doubleday had insisted that I take out several references to best-selling writers or famous personalities—such as my highlighting of several sadistic passages in Frank Slaughter's novel, *Divine Mistress*—Twayne wielded no blue pencil in this respect. They did object, however, to my dedicating the volume "to John Ciardi, one hell of a fine editor," insisting that this was not a dignified remark for a Ph.D. in psychology to make. I disagreed; but they won. Again, Lyle Stuart and Grove Press came to my rescue later by including the original dedication in the revised edition of the book.

My third book, *Sex Life of the American Woman and the Kinsey Report*, ran into serious censorship trouble again. Greenberg contracted to publish the work and then arranged with Popular Library to bring out a paperback edition simultaneously with their hardcover edition.

When Popular Library saw the manuscript of this anthology, they first rejected two of the chapters, one of which I had written on masturbation and another on prostitution with which I had collaborated with Dr. Harry Benjamin. Then, after further hemming and hawing, they reneged on their contract to publish the whole book, even though they had to sacrifice a substantial down payment by so doing.

Although Popular Library's objections, like those of Doubleday, were never made too explicit, it appeared that they ardently disliked the fact that *Sex Life of the American Woman* was largely pro-Kinsey and they were afraid that, as a paperback publisher, they might run into official censorship on the book.

Doubleday, out of similar fears, had deliberately overpriced *The Folklore of Sex*, the argument being that official agencies are less likely to ban a book that is high-priced than one that is low-priced. Actually, for all the publishers' caution in this connection, none of my publications has as yet aroused any official action, except when a paperback edition of *Sex Without Guilt* was banned, along with 99 other books (including novels by William Faulkner and John Steinbeck) in one county of Southern California.

Sex Life of the American Woman and the Kinsey Report was finally published in hard-backed form by Greenberg, a firm that itself took a highly liberal attitude toward the publication of sex material. As a result of legal advice, however, Greenberg omitted from the book the same two chapters that Popular Library had first banned.

My opinion, and that of my collaborators on the book, was that these chapters were not objectionable or censurable. We lost.

With my fourth book, *Sex, Society, and the Individual*, I

ran into no censorship problems as far as publication and editing were concerned for the simple reason that the book was published by Dr. A.P. Pillay, the coeditor of the book.

The *New York Times*, however, for several years refused to publish advertisements on this or any of my sex books—even if the ad contained nothing more than the title of the book and the name of the author. At first, large advertisers, who include scores of titles in each ad, were able to squeeze mentions of some of my volumes into their *Times* displays. But later even this privilege was denied all sex books that I authored.

When queried in this respect, the *Times* never came up with a satisfactory explanation—especially in view of the fact that it frequently publishes advertisements for more conservatively attuned sex volumes. Later, the *Times* ran ads on several of my sex books, but often insisted on cutting out large chunks of the ads submitted for them by the publishers.

With my fifth book on sexual topics, *The Psychology of Sex Offenders*, which was published by Charles Thomas, I encountered no censorship difficulties. Thomas is a medical publisher, and its editors did not object to a single word or sentence in the volume. And since the book was never published in a paperback edition or offered for display in the *New York Times* or any other popular paper or magazine, it managed to run into no censorship troubles.

Many of my subsequent works on sex, love, and marriage were published by Lyle Stuart, Inc.—largely because, after this firm brought out the first edition of *Sex Without Guilt*, I discovered that the same freedom of speech which permeated the columns of *The Independent* similarly prevails in Lyle's book publications. Although he has personally disagreed with some of my ultraliberal views, he has never red-penciled any of my frank expressions or expletives; and, so far, both of us have nicely managed to stay out of jail.

In any event, even though my most controversial books—including *Reason and Emotion in Psychotherapy, If This Be Sexual Heresy...*, *Sex and the Single Man, The Intelligent Woman's Guide to Dating and Mating*—and my hard-hitting sex manual, *The Art and Science of Love*, have all been published by Lyle Stuart, Inc. Even though reviewers have frequently uttered anguished screams about my ideas and language in these books, my censorship problems with them have been absolutely nil, which tends to show, I am convinced, that it is not usually the American public and our police forces that are our worst censoring agencies, but the publishers themselves.

Just to make this point even more convincing, I again had the same old censorship mish-mash when I arranged to have some sex books brought out by other publishers than Lyle Stuart. Bernard Geis commissioned me to do *The Intelligent Woman's Guide to Dating and Mating*, and liked the manuscript very much, but found my language "too rough." When I reluctantly agreed to tone some of it down so that the book would not be inordinately delayed in going to press, he finally decided that his main business associates (which included *Look* and *Esquire* magazines) would never tolerate the liberal sex views I included in the book, especially those outlined in a chapter on "The Fine Art of the Pickup." Although he predicted (with what subsequently turned out to be a goodly degree of accuracy) that the book would sell very well, he forfeited the advance royalty, returned the manuscript to me, and agreed to let me have—guess who!—publish it.

A little later on, I took another chance and let a publisher talk me (and my coauthor, Edward Sagarin) into doing a book called *Nymphomania: A Study of the Oversexed Woman*. Much to our chagrin, some of the material in the manuscript was bowdlerized as it was being rushed into print; and the sexiest chapter of the book, which was called "How to Satisfy a Nymphomaniac Sexually" and which had been specifically asked for by the original editor, was entirely deleted because it was "too provocative." Later, arrangements were made to include this chapter in another of my books—whose publisher, this time, thought it perfectly fine and proper.

With still another of my books—the massive, two-volumed *Encyclopedia of Sexual Behavior* which I edited in collaboration with Albert Abarbanel and which was published by MacMillan and Hawthorne—the contents of the articles themselves were not censored by the publisher (except, I believe, in some of the foreign countries where the *Encyclopedia* has been translated and republished); but great effort was brought to bear on me and my collaborator to include in the volumes several ultraconservative articles, since a number of our contributors were (without my instructing them to be) quite liberal in their presentations.

Having, by now, published more than 20 books on sex, love, and marriage, and having had considerable experience with many varieties of publishers, editors, reviewers, and advertising people, I am inclined to take a somewhat less than enthusiastic view of the many friends and fellow writers who greet me with some variation of "My God, aren't you lucky to be writing in the sex field. Such a popular area! And so much money to be made in it!"

Actually, this is largely bosh. Perhaps the cheap and sensational writers on sex or the mealymouthed romanticists sell their talents for a pretty penny, but the hardheaded, objective, straight-shooting purveyor of sex information is hardly in this boat. In fact, he or she is lucky to set sail at all.

It is my experience that today's authors who write honest sex books will, in the first place, have difficulty finding any publisher for their work. Then if they do find one, they will often have to fight their way through censorship difficulties with the publisher, editors, and lawyers. Then they will find that the public notices and reviews they receive rarely are commensurate in quantity or quality to those of non-sexual volumes which they may have published.

To make matters still worse, writers will often find that their book has been deliberately overpriced just because it deals with sex. They may be shocked to note that some of the finest bookstores refuse to display it prominently, especially in their windows. Many libraries will refuse to purchase the book; or else, when they do purchase it, put it on restricted shelves and discourage reader interest in it. Finally, their books may run into official or semi-official disapproval, and may be banned from advertising columns, from the mails, from public sale in certain communities, or, in extreme cases, from any further printings.

The one good break which the writers of sex books are likely to experience is to find that if and when their arduously produced and fought-for volume is finally remaindered—as it easily may be in dishearteningly record time—it is *then* likely to be prominently displayed in bookstores and advertisements—because, of course, it deals with S-E-X.

In view of these facts, most of which are often present in the United States, I am inclined to paraphrase the famous advice which *Punch* a century ago gave to men about to be married. Say I in this latter-day version: "Advice to authors who are about to write a sex book: Don't."

Having discussed some of my encounters with censorship in the course of writing and publishing books on sexual topics, I shall now continue this gory saga with a few of my adventures with other aspects of sex restriction. First, as to professional journals. You might not think that scientific journals, which presumably are devoted only to the publication of fact and truth, would be particularly squeamish about sex articles. But you might be surprised.

The International Journal of Sexology was valiantly and spiritedly edited by Dr. A.P. Pillay of Bombay, India. It had numerous brushes with sex censorship and was at times banned in several countries. Many years ago, when it was published under the name of *Marriage Hygiene*, its entry into the United States was barred, and a famous legal battle was fought, and won, on its behalf.

Nonetheless, although I was the American editor of the *Journal* and Dr. Pillay continually asked me to write papers for it, he refused to publish my article, "New Light on Masturbation," which is now printed in this book. He apologetically wrote me that such an outspoken article just could not be published in India, because it would offend the members of certain sectarian groups.

Another paper of mine—on masturbation among prisoners—was requested by the editor of *The Journal of Social Therapy*, the official publication of the Medical Correctional Association. Contrary to the usual procedure for scientific publication, I received no proofs on this article before it went to press. When I saw it in print, I was shocked to find that what I considered to be the most important and forceful paragraph in the paper, which forthrightly said that prison officials should, far from discouraging their charges from masturbating, be thankful that they have some normal sex outlet, was completely omitted.

After the journal containing this article had already been printed, the editor asked me whether I would like to have some corrections or additions made in it. I said that I certainly would; and that when the paper was reprinted, as it was supposed to be, in a monograph to be issued by the Federal Government as a handbook for prison officials, I would definitely like to see the *full* version published. Since then I have heard nothing from the editor—and nothing about the proposed monograph.

My experience with the editors of *Social Problems*, the official journal of the Society for the Study of Social Problems, was surprisingly similar—only worse. After the publication of the second Kinsey report, I was asked to contribute a paper on the report for a special issue of the journal, which was later to be republished in book form.

I wrote an article on "Female Sexual Response and Marital Relations" in which I showed that, whatever one may think of the Kinsey methodology, the last five chapters of *Sexual Behavior in the Human Female* are most important for an understanding of human sex relations. As usual, I minced few words about how, if they took the Kinsey material seriously, husbands and wives could employ extra-vaginal as well as vaginal techniques to achieve greater sex satisfaction.

Much to my displeasure, this article was considerably cut when it appeared in *Social Problems*—purely because, the editors, insisted, of "necessary space limitations." I soon discovered, however, that whereas my paper was cut to the bone, to become easily the shortest one published, several other papers, especially those which were thoroughly anti-Kinsey, were given plenty of space.

As in the case of the article in *The Journal of Social Therapy*, the editors of *Social Problems* asked me, *after* publication, whether I would like any changes or additions in the paper when it went into book covers. I immediately replied that I damned well would. Several months later, when the book had already gone to press, they phoned to tell me that, somehow, they had forgotten about my request to use the original version of my paper, and that it was now too late to do anything about it, so they would print the highly censored version.

But even this did not end the matter. A few weeks later, they called to say that the book had turned out to be too long and that therefore several papers, including mine, had to be dropped entirely. They were very sorry; but that's the way things were, and nothing could be done about it.

When the book actually appeared, under the title of *Sexual Behavior in American Society*, it proved to be a rather massive tome of 446 pages, which not only contained the original papers that had been published in the journal, but many other articles, virtually all of them anti-Kinsey, reprinted from various other sources. Conspicuously lacking, however, was only one paper from the original symposium—mine. Similarly, a paper I was asked to do for a text on criminality was found to contain too much sexy language in the therapeutic conversations I reported with actual offenders and was rejected.

So much for some of my encounters with professional publications. With popular magazines, my experience has been, as one might expect in this pressure-minded society, even more replete with sex censorship.

Time and again I have been called upon to prepare or outline articles by editors of mass circulation magazines, such as *Cosmopolitan* and the *Ladies Home Journal*. But although I think I may safely say that I am generally considered to be one of America's outstanding authorities on sexual subjects, for many years few of my down-to-earth essays in the field appeared in a large national magazine. My efforts were somehow always found to be "too realistic," "too bold for our readers" or "overly controversial." A footnote was originally inserted in the first edition of this book to the effect that *Esquire* had just broken the sex barrier by accepting one of my articles, *The Case for Polygamy*, for early publication. However, after paying me generously for the article, *Esquire* first delayed its publication and finally at the behest of one of the chief editors who found it "too strong," returned it to me. At the time the first edition of this book was published the escutcheon of any American mass circulation journal still remained completely unsullied by the inclusion of a sex article by the impure Dr. Albert Ellis.

When I finally did break into print in a small popular magazine, largely because the editor was a good friend of mine to whom I had given several ideas on what kind of periodical he might publish, he enthusiastically accepted my first article and vaguely said that he might change it around a bit. I thought, naturally, that he would consult me about these changes.

To my surprise, he blithely changed some of the salient points of my article without consulting me; and each change was a distinct toning-down of any liberal sex views I may have included. Thus, I asked, in the course of a discussion of sex freedom in marriage, "Can the average American couple practice sex freedom in marriage and still have a good marital relationship?" And I replied: "The answer is, alas, no." My editor friend changed this to: "The answer is, of course, a resounding no."

Since the publication of the first edition of this book, I have had more success than usual with publishing material in national magazines. *Pageant* has been the most liberal periodical in this respect, and has actually asked me to write and has printed four sex articles by me. Mass circulation magazines such as *Cosmopolitan* have also included pieces of my authorship. More often than not, however, such publications have been more interested in my non-sexual than my sexual writings; and when they have run the latter they have commonly deleted or changed significant passages where I was exceptionally frank about sex activities.

Even the highly sexy men's magazines have at times proved to be quite prissy in this regard. Thus, after I had written, on request, an article on nymphomania for *Gent* (which was one of the sexiest of the men's publications), the editor apologetically told me that he had to be very careful of post office regulations, and that I therefore had to delete all explicit references to sex relations that I had included in this article. And an article I wrote for another men's periodical, *Saga*, on "How to Have an Affair and End It with Style," was seriously cut and bowdlerized, without my consent, before it was printed.

Space does not permit the recounting of all my other brushes with restrictions on my written words on sex, so let me give some examples from the field of the spoken word.

I have often given talks on sexual topics, particularly to public forums, church, and community groups. Normally, I find that some members of my audience are somewhat startled, at the beginning of my talk, when I openly and unashamedly start using scientific sex terminology (such as "vagina," "penis," and "erection") and when I do not cavil about how my listeners can achieve greater sex satisfaction by ridding themselves of many of their taboos, superstitions, and sex prejudices.

After a few minutes of my talking this way, however, I invariably find that the members of the audience acquire, by a process of osmosis, some of my own lack of embarrassment and concern about unadulterated sexuality and become relaxed enough to enjoy, and even actively participate in, the discussion. After the formal presentation is over, many of them usually come up to speak to me informally, and sometimes keep me till far into the night or early morning.

If audience reaction is fine at these times, much less can be said for administrative response. For as soon as the sponsors of my sex talks get wind of what I may say, they frequently become most disturbed and block all efforts, which members of the audience often instigate, to have me return for further talks.

One of the most flagrant instances of administrative interference I have ever encountered occurred when I was talking to the members of a community group in the Bronx. The regular leader of the group had to leave before my speech was finished, but he left a specially chosen chairman in his place and, in addition, his wife to monitor the proceedings from a first-row vantage point.

I was talking, in this instance, about the contributions of modern sexual research to the husband-wife relationships. When the last word was hardly out of my mouth, the director's wife got up and made a twenty-minute peroration against almost everything I had said; and then, immediately after she finished, the chairman of the group, as if by a prearranged signal, himself gave a ten-minute speech which was largely directed against the points I had made, and he then adjourned the meeting.

Several members of the audience, incensed at the fact that I was not even given a chance to rebut my two speaking associates, rose to object to the peremptory manner in which the meeting was being closed. The chairman, broadly insinuating that the objectors were "violent liberals," ruffians, and blackguards, still closed the meeting. Sexual virtue, no doubt, once more triumphed.

After I wrote the first edition of *Sex Without Guilt*, I began to make more frequent radio and TV performances; and I quickly began to run into censorship trouble in this sensitive medium. When I spoke up in favor of premarital sex relations on a TV station in New York, such a hue and cry was raised that several years after that my appointment as a consultant in clinical psychology to the Veterans Administration was temporarily blocked because I had advocated "free love" on this particular program.

I appeared many times on the famous Long John Nebel radio show in New York, and the programs on which I appeared were very popular and were normally tape recorded and rebroadcasted at a later date. The program I did on *Sex Without Guilt*, however, in which masturbation and fornication were specifically mentioned as desirable sex acts, was forbidden to be rebroadcast by the station management.

On another station, I debated the virtues of premarital sex relations with the editor of a magazine (who strongly opposed such relations, although she was unmarried at this time and showed up at the station with a man who was obviously her lover). When I vigorously stated that a woman, to be mentally healthy, had damned well better stop caring too much what others thought of her sex reputation, the station received hundreds of protests. The Federal Communications Commission took the program off the air until the station explained that it had not specifically invited me to say what I said, and that I had made similar statements over many other radio and TV shows previously. The management of the station humbly apologized to its audience, the next day, for my appearance.

On the David Susskind "Open End" TV show, I appeared with Max Lerner, Hugh Hefner, Ralph Ginzburg, Maxine Davis, and Reverend Arthur Kinsolving, in a two-hour program entitled "The Sex Revolution." When David Susskind asked me, on this program, what I would do if I had a teenage daughter, and when I candidly said that I would encourage her to pet to orgasm rather than to have intercourse (because of the danger of pregnancy and disease involved in coitus), but that if she insisted on having full sex relations I would fit her up with a diaphragm or birth control pills and tell her to have fun, the program was banned from the Metropolitan Broadcasting syndicated TV network, and the two-hour TV tape of the program was never played anywhere. Ironically enough, Max Lerner, on the same show, had previously remarked that the mere fact that we were doing this program that night showed how liberal in its sex attitudes TV was becoming!

When I did a live daytime radio performance on CBS New York and clearly said on air that premarital sex relations were fine and that the Bible was hardly a great guide to sane sex conduct, more than a thousand listeners jammed the telephone lines to complain to the station about my sexual liberality; and the Federal Communications Commission again considered suspending this program from the air. When I said similar things on the telephone-answering shows on radio stations in Philadelphia, Boston, Los Angeles, and other cities, complaints were voluble and vociferous; and in consequence I am now persona non grata with several of these stations.

In recent years, a pernicious form of pre-censorship has

been applied to me by several radio and TV outlets. Thus, producers of some programs will call me and arrange to have me be on the air a week or two later. Then, just before the program is about to be recorded or to go on live, they will call me again and give some lame excuse why they cannot use me on the show, or else will honestly admit that they have been told that I am "too controversial" and that therefore someone connected with the program objects to my being on it.

As a result of these various types of sex censorship, my participation in radio and TV programs in New York City and throughout the country have been seriously curtailed in recent years; and I sometimes wonder if eventually practically all the large and respectable outlets will be barred to me. If so, I shall just have to keep writing more articles and books than ever!

To this day, there is much discrimination against me for my liberal sex views, my pioneering use of four-letter words in my speeches and writings, and my sexual honestly. I am probably the most famous living psychologist, and have been voted the most influential theorist and practitioner by American and Canadian counselors and psychologists. I have been given the highest professional and scientific awards offered by the American Psychological Association, the American Counseling Association, the Association for the Advancement of Behavior Therapy, and several other leading national associations, as well as the Humanist of the Year Award from the American Humanist Association. I have also published more full-length professional and public books and articles than any other psychologist, including a number of best-selling volumes. I have set records for professional and public workshops, talks, and other presentations in New York City, many other American cities, and several foreign countries. I am also the founder of Rational Emotive Behavior Therapy, the first of the now influential cognitive behavior therapies.

For these and other reasons, I obviously have a considerable degree of recognition and renown. Nevertheless, I think that I am still censored and discriminated against largely because of my well-known liberal attitudes about sex. For example, here are a few of the instances in which my sex views got me into difficulty:

I was scheduled to be President-Elect of the American Academy of Psychotherapists, the American Association of Marital & Family Therapists, and the Division of Psychotherapy of the American Psychological Association, but at the last minute, arrangements somehow got unscheduled.

I was going to give a two-day workshop for professionals in Rational Emotive Behavior Therapy at North Texas State University, but members of the Board of Directors of the University got wind of my workshop a week in advance and made sure it was cancelled. Several other universities that arranged for me to speak on therapy, and not on sex topics, also cancelled my appearances when members of their faculty objected to my liberal sex views.

I was scheduled to appear on several leading TV shows, including Oprah and the Johnny Carson Show; but just before the shows were to be broadcast, I was found to be "too controversial" and my appearances were cancelled.

I was to be the main invited speaker and workshop presenter at the annual conferences of several important regional psychological and counseling associations, but was finally uninvited because some people on the arranging boards made a fuss about my published sex attitudes.

So it has gone; and so do I expect it to go in my years

to come. Sex frankness often breeds sex suppression. This will not stop me from continuing to write things about sex that had better be said and written. But—to be realistic—it will definitely curb and limit me in this respect.

That is too bad; but, fortunately, not fatal.

8

How Men Contribute to Women's Sexual Inadequacy

M uch of women's sexual inadequacy that I have seen in my clinical practice has been either directly or indirectly caused by male ideas and practices.

Much of the so-called "coldness" I hear about, in fact, turns out to be nothing of the sort: since many women who come to complain that they are sexually unorgasmic turn out to be, on closer questioning, fully as capable of orgasm as are their male consorts—and frequently more so. But their *notions* of their sex capacities are so distorted and warped that they imagine an incompetence that they do not truly have; and these misperceptions are often derived from similar ideas believed in and propagated by presumably sophisticated males.

In our society, males cause and abet female "inadequacy" in several major ways. First, by constructing a theory of female orgasm that, while neatly designed to bolster the male ego, has little or nothing to do with the facts of female behavior.

Thus, therapists like Sigmund Freud, reasoning that young girls masturbate by manipulating their external sex organs (particular their clitoris) and that older women often obtain a climax through having sexual intercourse, concluded that the normal woman *should* be satisfied through having coitus, and that if she is not she is sexually immature or neurotic.

Theories about women's inadequacy are all very interesting and seemingly logical. The trouble is that, in the case of literally millions of women, they simply do not work.

Curiously enough, in spite of all the male hullabaloo about how females *should* have so-called vaginal orgasms in order to be sexually "mature" or "fulfilled," the fact remains that many women, in the course of their entire lives, rarely or never *do* experience this kind of climax.

However, many of these vaginally "frigid" women not only obtain perfectly satisfactory orgasms all their lives, but regularly obtain more frequent, more intense, and more lasting climaxes than do many males.

Why, then, do males emphasize the *right* way that a female *should* achieve orgasm? Jealousy of women's greater prowess in this area? Perhaps. Unwillingness to accord women true equality of sexual status? Possibly. More to the point, however, seems to be an even simpler explanation: namely, that because the *male* is very nicely satisfied with vaginal intromission, or coitus, he thinks that it is only cricket that the female should *also* be. And when, as is often true, she is not, but turns out to possess another organ of satisfaction, the clitoris, which affords *him*, the male, relatively little satisfaction, he simply cannot bring himself to understand *why* this should be.

So he quickly dreams up, and dogmatically writes up in textbooks, theories which conclusively "prove" that any woman who, unlike most men, does not specifically enjoy and have a terrific orgasm during vaginal copulation is unquestionably "immature," "peculiar," or "disturbed." The sorriest part of this game is that when these obviously male-centered ideas become sufficiently repeated and endlessly quoted they soon take on the aura no longer of speculative theory but of indubitable "fact."

As a result, not only males but millions of women start to believe the never-proven "validity" of vaginal orgasm, and become so disturbed by not having their climaxes as they are theoretically *supposed* to have them that some finally throttle them completely and become incapable of obtaining either vaginal or extravaginal intense sensations. Their consequent "frigidity" is then taken as evidence in proof of the original hypothesis that they are just neurotic women!

A core of many female sex problems in our society, then, is the masculine attitude that because males are easily satisfied in coitus, females should *also* be. This leads to an almost automatic corollary: namely, that males who believe this theory often have poor sexual technique. At the best, they are aware of several sex methods and variations that result in fairly rapid satisfaction for themselves; at the worst, they insist on one quick, preliminaryless form of intercourse (usually with the male surmounting the female in the face to face position), and that is that.

In either event, these coitus-fixated males rarely recognize the female desire for preliminary love-making, including clitoral and vaginal stimulation with other parts of their anatomy than their sacred penises. And in those instances where they do attempt nonpenile contacts with their partners, they are still shocked by the idea that these contacts should often, and with some women always, be continued up to and including their partner's climax.

When the males of our society finally acknowledge that

there is nothing sacred about intercourse, and that there are several *other* legitimate means of heterosexual satisfaction, they still, for the most part, insist on seeing nonpenile and nonvaginal contacts as necessarily *preliminary* ones—preliminary, of course, to coitus. The fact that extracoital contacts may, in, of, and by themselves, be very fulfilling and rewarding—this obvious fact of human sex anatomy and physiology is generally relegated to oblivion, and sometimes put under the rubric of "perversion" or "abnormality."

Actually, as I show elsewhere in this book, sexual "perversion" or "neurosis" is largely a fiction and, if it exists at all, does not consist of an individual's having noncoital sex acts, but of his or her having *any* kind of sexual participation, including coitus, on an exclusive, fixated, rigid, or self-defeating basis.

To round out the business of helping females in our culture to have little orgasmic pleasure, many males are aware that their female partners cannot and preferably should not be satisfied only through intercourse; and they know that noncoital sex techniques are not correctly to be labeled "perversions" or "abnormalities."

Still, because they do not want to take the relatively little time and trouble necessary to satisfy their partners in extra-coital ways, they consistently refuse to do so. Yet, these same men tend to be horribly shocked when their mates do not have dinner ready on time, or neglect mending their socks, or are late to a dinner date. They are often irritable when their partners would like them to cooperate in helping them come to orgasm, and woe and betide these same partners if they are vaginally unreceptive when these males decide that their abstinence of the last two days has gone much too far!

Because myriads of men in our society insist that

women absolutely *should* be sexually satisfied solely through coitus; because these men frequently make very poor lovers; and because they are often quite sexually selfish themselves while expecting their partners to be fully receptive whenever the spirit moves these males, there exist millions of women who, in spite of their having fine capacities for sex satisfaction, actually are sexually anesthetic with men. Betty Dodson has pointed out this sorry reality for almost 30 years, as of course have I. But it still exists!

In my own psychological practice, I find many women who come for help largely because they consider themselves "frigid" and discover, after I have seen them (and often their husbands) for a few weeks or months, that their sexual capacities easily exceed that of the average male. One thirty-year-old woman, who had been married for ten years, came because her husband kept complaining that she did not enjoy sex relations and did not seem to achieve orgasm. After considerable questioning, I determined that she usually did achieve a climax in sex relations, but that it was so slight and inconsequential that she hardly knew that she was having one.

Further questioning elicited the fact that this woman was so petrified by her husband's demands that she derive great satisfaction from intercourse that she actually derived little or no satisfaction from it. My dialogue with her proceeded in this manner:

Therapist: So every time you have intercourse with your husband, you are worried about how you are going to behave during it, about how you are going to react to it—is this correct?

Client: Yes. I keep wondering whether or not I'll have a climax, and whether he will be pleased.

Therapist: But that's exactly the thing to make sure that you will *not* have an orgasm!

Client: You mean that I block myself in this manner?

Therapist: That's just exactly what I mean. *Anyone* who does *anything* with anxiety tends to block herself from doing it adequately or well. Anyone who worries about *how* she is doing, instead of concentrating on *what* she is doing, easily diverts herself from the real problem at hand and performs poorly.

Client: Why is that?

Therapist: It's a simple matter of diversion, or lack of proper focusing. The human brain, somewhat like a calculating machine, actually seems to concentrate well on only one thing at a time. Even when you listen to music and read, you are usually not doing either act particularly well, but are wavering somewhat between the music and the reading matter. Isn't that so?

Client: Well, uh, I think I see what you mean. When I listen to music, really listen to it that is, I often can read a whole page without knowing what is on it. And when I concentrate on the reading, I hardly know what music is playing.

Therapist: Exactly. Well, other human performances, including sex acts, are often like that. If you concentrate or focus clearly on A, you don't focus too well on B; and *vice versa*.

Client: So if I concentrate on what my husband is thinking about my sexual performance, I can't, at the same time, focus too well on actually performing—is that it?

Therapist: That's just it. As long as you worry about how well you're doing sexually—which really means how well you're doing in your husband's eyes—you will find it difficult to think about what you are doing—which should be, of course, enjoying yourself.

Client: But what about my husband?

Therapist: Well, what about him?

Client: I—I mean, uh, what about his pleasure? What about his wanting me to have an orgasm?

Therapist: That, I am afraid, is *his* problem. Naturally, he will find it more satisfying, in many instances, if you fully enjoy sex. And he preferably should help you try to enjoy it. But is his harping on your getting an orgasm every time helping you in any way?

Client: No; quite the contrary.

Therapist: And is it helping *him*?

Client: No, I guess it isn't. He's just getting disgruntled and disappointed when I don't have a climax.

Therapist: All right, then: his harping on and worrying too much about *your* orgasm isn't helping you and isn't helping him. Obviously, then, he'd better stop his senseless worry, and it is his problem if he doesn't. By all means, let him get help, then, with his problem.

Client: But shouldn't he want me to have satisfaction?

Therapist: Yes, he should *want* it—but not *require* it. He should *prefer* your having a terrific sex climax, but not have a *dire need* of your having one. After all, if you don't have one, it's mainly your loss, isn't it, rather than his?

Client: Yes, but what of his ego?

Therapist: Ego? You mean, don't you, his *lack of ego?* If he had true ego-strength, or unconditional self-acceptance, he wouldn't *need* to keep bolstering it by showing himself how good he was at giving you sex pleasure. But because he doesn't like himself well enough, doesn't have enough acceptance of his *own*, he has to keep proving to himself how "good" he is by showing his ability to give *you* an orgasm. What kind of strength is that?

Client: Not very good, I guess.

Therapist: No, not very good at all. But that, as I say, is his problem, and he'd better get help with it. If he wants to talk to me about it, I'll be glad to talk to him; otherwise, he can see some other competent therapist. But let's get back to *your* problem.

Client: Yes, let's.

Therapist: Your problem is not, really, what your husband thinks about your having an orgasm but what *you* think about his thinking about your having it.

Client: I didn't quite get that.

Therapist: Let me repeat: Your problem, like anyone's problem, is practically never what another person thinks or does, but what *you* think about what he thinks or does.

Client: So if I don't care too much about what another, about what my husband, thinks or does, then I don't have a problem?

Therapist: That's right. At least, you don't have a neurotic problem; but you may have the original problem in its own right. Take your so-called "frigidity," for example. If you don't care too much, worry too much about your husband's attitude toward it, you will not be needlessly troubled—or what we call neurotic. *Then*, when you have overcome your neurosis in this connection, you can go back to considering the *real* problem—which, as I said before, is mainly how *you* can enjoy yourself sexually.

Client: And you think I can solve that problem, that real problem, if I stop concentrating on the false problem, the one my husband is creating by his worrying too much about my having an orgasm?

Therapist: I am reasonably sure that you can. If you stop worrying about his worries, and mainly concentrate when you have sex relations, on your own sex and love feelings, on what excites and satisfies you, then you will probably find it easy to have much more gratification than you are now having.

This client did, thereafter, concentrate on her own sex-love pleasures when she was having relations with her husband, and within a few more weeks she was getting stronger and stronger reactions. Two months after she first came for therapy, she was not only having intense climaxes most of the time she had intercourse, but was also having three or four terrific climaxes a night—while her husband, quite amazed, could not keep up with her coitally, and had to resort to extracoital methods of satisfying her on most occasions.

This, then, is what I often find clinically, but what I would be far more pleased, in our culture, *not* to keep finding—if only our males would stop contributing to female "frigidity," and if only our females would stop taking them, in this respect, too seriously.

What can men in our culture do to encourage, rather than often sabotage, women to enjoy more nonorgasmic and orgasmic sex? If you are a heterosexual male or a gay woman and want to enhance your partners' sexual functioning, you can get excellent instruction from a number of manuals, such as those listed in the references at the back of this book. Read them and get your partner's permission to experiment to see which recommended techniques actually work best with her. Some almost certainly will—and some won't. Experiment! Keep experimenting!

Don't forget that your sex-love *attitudes* are at least as good as, and often more useful than, your "best" techniques. But techniques are not to be neglected! Some of the "great" ideas and methods you can try are these?

1. Every woman is an individual and a member of the female sex, so what may be sauce for *one* goose may be ketchup or vinegar for another. Many or most women may thrill to one kind of sex (e.g., clitoral massage) but not *all* women all of the time.

2. Women, as sex manuals will tell you, *generally* are turned on by sex *plus* love, by affection, by romance, or by some reasonable facsimile of caring. Not, again, all women all of the time. A few sexpots *hate* love. But only a few.

3. Don't think that women, like most *males*, dote on a man's having a huge stiff cock. Some find it painful and some even like it soft or medium hard.

4. The more you think that you *absolutely must* give a woman terrific orgasms with your sacred penis, the more that penis is likely to go on strike. For *some* women (or *some* gay men), that would be *preferable*,

but hardly *necessary*. Anxiety about the functioning of your penis stems from your *demand* that it absolutely *must* function as you—and presumably your partner, too—*think* it must.

5. When your penis simply refuses to be as hard as you (and presumably your partner) would like it to be, remember that you almost always have several *other* non-coital ways of satisfying your woman (or gay) partner.

6. Unless you unconditionally accept yourself in spite of your sex (and other) failings, your women (and gay) partners will have difficulty accepting you. USA (unconditional self-acceptance) means that you *always* accept your total *self*, your *essence*, your *being*—no matter how "poor" or "bad" or "ineffective" your (sexual and non-sexual) acts are. USA won't *make* you wealthier, better looking, or sexier. But it will reduce your anxiety and depression and thereby *help* you function better. It also gives you self-confidence that tends to be attractive to your partners (and other people) and is therefore one of the most valuable characteristics you can possess.

7. Remember that just about *all* men can't get or maintain a stiff erection at all times and give up the idea that you are *uniquely* impotent at times while all other males are invariably hard as a baseball bat. Like hell they are! Also rid yourself of the notion that most other men can quickly and easily get two or more erections an evening after they have their first orgasm. Only some *lucky* ones can!

8. As some sages have remarked many centuries ago, your main erogenous zone is your brain—and, especially, your thinking. As Erick Janssen and his research asso-

ciates have recently experimentally found, your sexual arousal can be automatic *and* the result of controlled cognitive processes. You can often create and maintain your arousal by consciously thinking and imagining sexy stimuli that (sometimes) work for you. Experimentally find them and use them. But accept—not like—the fact that your most sexy thoughts at times do *not* work. Alas!

9. Don't think that William Masters and Virginia Johnson invented sex therapy in their 1970 book *Human Sexual Inadequacy*. They studied the findings of a good many ancient and modern sex therapists, including my writings of the 1940s, 1950s, and 1960s, and—like I did—rejected most of the Freudian theories of sex failure, and came up with several therapeutic methods that were based on solid research. They particularly solidified the idea that Alfred Kinsey had stressed in 1948 and 1953—that penile-vaginal intercourse is only *one* method you can take to satisfy yourself and your partners. Always keep this idea in mind! As behavior therapist Barry Bass recently noted, "Sexual dysfunction is the inevitable consequence of our futile efforts to attain sexual performance perfection." Yes, but you can *surrender* that idea!

10. You can investigate and use several "spiritual" and "transformational" methods of adding to your sex practices, including Tantra meditations, that were originated and taught almost 4,000 years ago. They can prolong your sex arousal and can enhance you and your partner's enjoyment in some instances. *Some*. But many highly sexed people—including myself—find that "spiritual" sex methods take considerable time and

effort to learn and add little to the great pleasure of "raw" sex. Tantra and other "spiritual" kinds of sex can also become obsessive-compulsive, time-consuming, and can *detract* you from the joys of down-to-earth sex. Try them, if you will, and see if they work for you. One young REBT practitioner who thoroughly enjoyed "plain sex" with his lover told me that when he persuaded her for several weeks to try tantric and other meditative kinds of sex, she found it "perfectly boring." As the French say, "Chacun à son goût!"—each one to her and his taste. If you hang yourself up on the "best" kind of sex, it may—for you—turn out to be one of the "worst."

9

Sexual Inadequacy in the Male

What the exact figures on male sexual inadequacy are no one, at present, knows. But judging from all existing indications, the chances are that they are enormous. My own estimate, from detailed questioning of many hundreds of clients and other people, is that millions of American men are much less sexually enjoying than they theoretically could be.

Sexual inadequacy in the male takes several main forms: (1) general lack of desire; (2) reaching a climax too rapidly (fast ejaculation); (3) inability to maintain an erection; (4) inability to achieve a climax; and (5) general inhibition, leading to the inability to fully enjoy sex and to satisfy female partners.

According to most psychological and sexological texts, these kinds of male inadequacy are often not based on physical deficiencies but stem from a male's emotional disturbances. In general, this is true, although it must be acknowledged that physical causes, such as biochemical imbalances, disease processes, and general physical disability, play an important part in some sexual malfunctionings.

It is also true, as textbooks often say, that some cases of

sexual impotence and anesthesia result from a man's deep-seated, long-standing neurotic tendencies, including unresolved early prejudices, underlying hostility against women, unconscious hatred of a particular female partner, and so on.

Nevertheless, I have found in clinical practice that most male sex disabilities take a generalized neurotic pattern and that this pattern is similar to the pattern of nonsexual disturbance which so many members of our populace, male and female, have. More specifically: I find that most cases of male inadequacy are caused by a general fear-of-failure pattern of behavior rather than by some special sex problem.

The fear-of-failure pattern works along the following lines: (1) A man feels that he *should* and *must* be good at some activity, such as sexual intercourse. (2) He fears that he will *not* be good at it, and that his failure will make him a thoroughly inadequate person. (3) Because of his fears, and because of the fact that all humans fail from time to time, he experiences actual failure several times. (4) This convinces him that he really *is* incompetent at this activity and *in general*. (5) He then begins to become more and more anxious about his performance; and, because of his anxiety, to perform less and less well. (6) A distinct vicious circle is thereby established: fear of failure leads to actual failure which in turn leads to more fear of failure.

Add to this fear-of-failure pattern the fact that, in our society, men's sex performances are made sacred and are not discussed openly, and chaos often results.

For if you are afraid to fail at anything—let us say, for example, swimming—the best way to get over your fear is to keep practicing the thing you fear—to swim and swim and swim. But how can one who is afraid of sexual failure practice sex when, both premaritally and postmaritally, he is most likely to be hemmed in with every possible kind of self-imposed, partner-imposed, and society-imposed restriction? How can he, with our terrific sex taboos, even honestly face the fact that he has a sex problem—as, say, he would face the fact that he had a swimming problem?

At every turn, the male in our culture who is sexually inadequate and who wants to overcome his inadequacy runs up against social restrictions and pressures.

How so? Let us suppose that you, a male reader of this book, feel some sexual inadequacy. What are some of the things you can do to overcome it? Try these procedures:

First of all rid yourself of the idea that the one "proper" and "normal" way of satisfying your partner is with your sacred penis. As I indicate in other chapters of this book, women are frequently not satisfied by sexual intercourse alone; and even when they are, it is a rare male who can satisfy the fully healthy, sexually released woman coitally, for the good reason that whereas the average man is capable of having intercourse several times a week, many women are capable of having it several times a day. If you exclusively rely on your penis to fulfill the sex needs of a moderately sexed woman, you are often doomed to failure at the start. Yet in our society, if you start thinking, as you'd better think, of non-coital means of satisfying your partner, you run against age-old superstitions and blockings. Gay men, too, over-emphasize the importance of penile size and power.

Second, if you want to better your lot, begin to look upon failures as normal and to accept the fact that none of us are perfect—especially as we grow older. You will often run into the general competitive mores of our culture, which loudly, if quite falsely, proclaim that everyone should be better than everyone else at everything he does, and that

everyone should always better his own previous performances. With competitive philosophies like this being ceaselessly drummed into your head, sexually failing will help
you berate yourself, thereby making yourself *more* anxious
and inept.

Third, if you begin to have some sex difficulties, you
can learn to control your thinking while having sex relations. If you suffer from fast ejaculation, you can learn to
think of sexually non-exciting things while having intercourse; and if you suffer from inability to maintain an erection or achieve an orgasm, you can think of sexually arous-
ing images and to try sex acts that are particularly exciting
to you.

Here our societal sex taboos again rise up to smite you:
since you are often taught that some of the sex acts which
you should execute to maintain your best performance are
"immoral" or "perverted" or "abnormal." And, believing
this nonsense, you may refuse to let yourself go sexually—
and consequently remain inadequate.

Fourth, as previously noted, the best way to eliminate
any fear is to do the thing you fear over and over: to gain
more and more practice at it. But, in our society, for a sexually competent individual to keep having steady sex relations is often the most difficult thing in the world.

If you are unmarried, we make sex practice quite difficult to achieve; and if you are married, we make it depend
almost entirely on the goodwill and lack of disturbance of
your wife. In either event, what generally happens is that
you, as a not too adequate male, finally become, from lack
of experience, more inadequate.

Finally, sex failure can be overcome if you conquer your
general inhibitions, throw yourself fully into the sex acts
you perform, and show your partners that you believe sex

is fine for both of you and that they preferably should make every effort to enjoy it to the utmost.

This, more specifically, involves your frankly talking with your partner about your sex desires, candidly discussing the times when you fail, and openly planning better procedures for future sex. But this kind of verbal and active uninhibitedness, again, is definitely discouraged in our antisexual culture, and can only be achieved by those who defy this culture, to some extent, rather than those who rigidly conform to it.

To sum it up, most male sexual inadequacy in our society is caused not so much by deep-seated, particularized psychological disturbances as by a more generalized fear of failure on one hand and sexual Puritanism on the other. Then, when men become embroiled in a vicious circle of fear of failure inciting to actual failure which in turn produces further anxiety, they have difficulty overcoming their increasing sexual inadequacy. Because society, once again, sets up barriers of competitiveness and antisexuality that make it difficult for men to do much about their sexual incompetence. By *this* time, they are often so disturbed by their boxed-in and seemingly hopeless condition that they develop a full-blown neurosis.

The solution?

As usual, there is no perfect solution within the framework of the present social order. Some individuals can distinctly be helped by going for psychotherapy—which, when it is effectively done, will help them adjust to the inadequacies of their culture by selectively accepting and ignoring certain of its rigid dictates. Also: by discovering that they have their own innate and learned tendencies to take their healthy preferences to do well sexually (and otherwise) and to satisfy their partners but then to unhealthfully escalate them into three absolutist *musts, shoulds,* and *oughts*: (1) "I *must* perform well sexually and win my partner's love and approval!" (2) "Other people *must* give me sexually (and otherwise) exactly what I want!" (3) "World conditions under which I live must be good and comfortable, else I *can't stand* it and be happy at all!"

To be more specific than I have so far been in this chapter, what can men do about their own sexual inadequacy—or about what they *see* as their "inadequacy"? Answer: Reread the ten points I make at the end of the chapter before this one. Then, as you read these points about how you can stop yourself from helping your woman partners to feel sexually inadequate, apply them to your own feelings of inadequacy. Thoroughly review how "sexually inadequate" you really are, and give up your unrealistic notions of being *perfectly* adequate. What man ever was? Maybe Adam. Who since his time? Not you! Or me!

What can you women (or gay male) readers of this book do to stop helping your male sex partners to overcome their beliefs in their sexual inadequacy? Again, reread the ten points I make at the close of the previous chapter and give some deep thought to how they can apply to you and your partners. Okay, do it now!

Here, in addition, are some other ideas and techniques you can use to encourage your male partners to surrender their ideas that they are "sexually inadequate."

First, even slightly hinting that you *need* your male to have a large stiff cock and to mightily wield it in your sensitive orifices. You'd *like* that to (sometimes) happen; but you by no means *need* it. Show your male that there are several *other* ways for him to sexually—and lovingly—satisfy you.

At the same time, show your male partner that you can

definitely arouse him and usually bring him to orgasm without vaginal or anal intercourse. If you haven't found them yet, explore and experiment.

Show your partner that *two* of your main goals are to please him sexually and to have him bring you to arousal and orgasm. But they are not your *only* goals. Often show him that his companionship, support, understanding, partnership, and other nonsexual elements are quite desirable.

Give your partner unconditional other-acceptance (UOA). Accept him *as is*, as a person, in spite of your recognizing his (sexual and nonsexual) faults and limitations. Use some of the methods that I and Ted Crawford describe in *Making Intimate Connections* to achieve an unangry, caring, valuable relationship with him. Especially use revolving discussion sequence (RDS).

If your sexual (and nonsexual) relationship with your partner continues to be unsatisfying and perhaps disruptive, consult with a professional counselor or therapist.

10

When Are We Going to Quit Stalling About Sex Education?

More nonsense is written about sex education than about virtually any other popular subject. In spite of these writings, or perhaps in some measure because of them, American sex attitudes, as I have shown for many years, are thoroughly confused.

Thus, we heartily believe in sex education—and do little or nothing about it.

We say that we should go all out to teach our children the facts of life—and then, in our sex education materials, delete many of its realistic facts.

We put on determined sex education campaigns—and then see that our young people are so abysmally ignorant that they undergo numerous unwanted pregnancies, unnecessary abortions, forced marriages, gruesome wedding nights, great sex fears, and needless divorces.

The truth is that our sex education today is bound to be emasculated, for the simple reason that our *general* sex beliefs are inconsistent and muddled. Most of us are not even aware of our now-you-see-them-and-now-you-don't sex attitudes, as their deepest roots are often unconscious rather than conscious. Typically, we *seem* to think one way about sex but actually *think* quite another.

For example, we are consciously horrified by the thought of premarital sex relations and adultery, yet we unconsciously envy, laugh with, and even applaud fornicators and adulterers. Or we consciously think abortion is permissible—and still castigate ourselves for having or aiding with one.

When, with our many open and underlying sex conflicts, we try to teach our children the scientific facts of sex, we inevitably fumble pretty badly. We want to be oh so casual and cool about conveying the facts of life; instead, we tend to stammer, blush, look out of the window, paw restlessly at the floor with our feet, or otherwise avoid coming to direct, matter-of-fact terms with the subject we are trying to present. But children, of course, sense our feelings as well as our words. And telling them that sex is a perfectly natural and beautiful part of life while you are humhawing to beat all get-out is like trying to persuade them that you love your mother-in-law while you are using her picture as a spit target.

Let's face it: good sex education needs good sex teachers—teachers who are themselves free from irrational taboos; who think that sex is often good clean fun; who preferably have had a fine and abundant sex life themselves; and who can handle their own sex problems in much the same manner as they solve nonsexual life situations.

These teachers, whether they be parents or professionals, should of course present sex education in a global, total-pattern manner, as part of a unified picture of life. Human sex behavior cannot be divorced from emotion, personality, social living, economic affairs, and the other complex aspects of modern living. Sex educators should not, under the guise of placing the facts of sex in the general context of life, instill irrelevant, guilt-producing ideas that will pietistically obscure the facts.

No one, for example, would begin to teach a child homemaking tasks and responsibilities by beginning: "The home is a sacred place, and cooking and cleaning are beautiful God-given acts that must always be carried out seriously and soberly so that the fundamental purposes of life may be gloriously fulfilled." Yet, this is the kind of hokum with which our books and talks on sex education are commonly filled.

Naturally, when handed this type of "enlightenment," bright children quickly begin to wonder what it is about sex that is so intrinsically filthy that mealy-mouthed words by the dozen are needed to help clean it up.

Once again: our children are virtually never taught that playing baseball is a worthy pastime—but that you must not talk about it publicly. Or that reading is an estimable occupation—but that *book, hero,* and *read* are nasty four-letter words which you must never say aloud. Or that playing chess is a wonderful sport—providing that you do not play it with your mother, father, sister, brother, other blood relations, any member of your own sex, and that you play it with only one member of the other sex in your entire lifetime. Yet, while smugly assuring our youngsters that sex is the finest and most beautiful thing in the world, we seriously caution them not to engage in, speak about, or ever privately think about it—except, perhaps, on any Fourth of July that happens to fall on Monday of a leap year. And then we wonder why, as adolescents and adults, they happen to have numerous sex problems!

Not all sex educators are rigidly puritanical by any means. Unusual ones, like Sol Gordon and Judith Levine, go out of their way to be especially courageous in their pro-sexual views—as I particularly mention in my final chapter of this book. Modern sex manuals—such as Alex Comfort's

The Joy of Sex and Betty Dodson's *Orgasms for Two*—do a fine job of sexually educating many adults.

In the area of educating children, however, we have some unbelievable sexual censorship and restrictions. Consider the case of JoAnn Hamilton, which was described by a reporter, Michael Janofsky, in the *New York Times* on February 2, 2003. Mrs. Hamilton, according to Janofsky's story, is a 64-year-old Mormon mother of 8, stepmother of 13, and foster mother of sixteen children. She has campaigned for years in Bountiful, Utah to shield children from "pornography." What kind of pornography? All kinds!

Even popular magazine pictures of models in swimsuits "can lead boys to sexual addiction and arrested emotional development." So Mrs. Hamilton did—and still does—her best to help prosecutors like Paula Houston, who had the job of "obscenity and pornography complaints ombudsman" in a prosperous Utah community.

The sex censorship efforts of Mrs. Hamilton, Janofsky reports, have made her "a heroine to many friends and neighbors." She has got hundreds of people to post signs on their lawns that say "Protect Children: Remove Inappropriate Material from View." What is inappropriate material? It seems to be almost *any* suggestive magazine covers and inside photos and stories. Store owners are forced to remove the *National Enquirer* and other tabloids from checkout counters; to wrap the covers of magazines like *Cosmopolitan* and *Vogue* "to hide any hint of sexuality;" and, as the manager of a popular market in Bountiful reported, "Anything that's lewd, like women's busts showing cleavage, or bad remarks, we cover up so only the name shows." Not only is this rampant sex censorship, but it resides in a prosperous American community in the twenty-first century. By comparison, some of our New England seventeenth century puritans seem tame!

What, then, is the answer?

Very frankly, as I pointed out in *The Case for Sexual Liberty*, there is no perfect, or even half-perfect, answer. Societal sex attitudes must be extensively changed before we can reasonably expect specific sex education to be effective.

If you, for example, managed to surmount your own sex biases to some extent, and to present your child with scientific sex viewpoints, you would be producing a youngster who would largely be out of step with his own community, since it is most unlikely that many of the other parents in your region would have given their children a similar sexual frame of reference. The result would be that your youngster, while he might well be less sexually disturbed than his peers, would still tend to suffer from the disturbances of his environment: a sorry, and none the less incontrovertible, fact to contemplate.

Is the case of sex education in present-day America entirely hopeless then? No, not entirely. On the practical side, there are still a few things you can do to help along the cause of honest-to-goodness sex education in this and succeeding generations. Here are some suggestions:

1. Recognize your own sex ignorance and limitations and do not pretend that you know what you obviously do not know about sex and love.

2. Read as many factual books and articles on sex as you can—and read everything that you read critically. Ignore opinions that are moralistic or sectarian and try to draw conclusions from data rather than dogma. Try to recognize much of the sexual ignorance and prejudices of your community and the world, such as those indicated in this chapter and in chapters 6, 12, and 15.

3. Face your own sex problems squarely and honestly—

and run, do not walk, to the nearest psychologist or marriage counselor when you are sexually disturbed.

4. As soon as your children begin asking sex questions, answer them in a direct, factual, down-to-earth manner. Teach them that sex, in virtually all its aspects, is a fine, pleasurable thing. But also teach them that the world is full of bigots who think otherwise and who will try to make them feel guilty about their sexuality. Tell them that, unfortunately, they will often have to obey laws against public displays of sexuality—but as long as they are discreet, they can, in the privacy of their thoughts and boudoirs, guiltlessly keep their own counsels.

5. If you have any qualms about giving proper sex education to your children, do not hesitate to call on other qualified persons to help you do so. Psychologists, physicians, marriage counselors, teachers, and others who have specialized in sex education will be glad to be of service.

6. Above all, try to be accepting, non-critical, and democratic about the sex behavior of others. Take the same attitudes toward sex ethics and morals as you would toward general ethics and morals. Work, in whatever way you can, for rules and laws that seek only to discourage sex acts where one individual needlessly, gratuitously, and distinctly harms another, rather than statues and mores based on superstition, ignorance, and sadistic sex "morality." When your children or others commit what you consider "wrong" or "bad" sex acts, do your best to give them unconditional other-acceptance (UOA)—that is, to sometimes object (unangrily) to their *behaviors* but do not damn *them*, as persons, for their actions.

11

On the Myths About Love

Many myths about love are wittingly or unwittingly promoted in our newspapers, magazines, radio and TV shows, films, novels, songs, and other mass media. Indeed because of the romantic attitudes encouraged by these media, it may well be held that they usually contain more poetry than truth.

In consequence, perhaps the vast majority of Americans experience a love life that is remarkable for its mediocrity. Even some of their most significant amours tend to be so shallow that they add relatively little to the enhancement of their living.

Some of the myths about love which are most prevalent in our culture are these:

The myth that love is mysterious and that no one knows what it is.

Love, actually, is definable in simple terms. It is a human evaluation or emotion—and, like all emotion, a biased perception of something that leads one to react strongly to it in a favorable (or unfavorable) way.

Love arises when you evaluate something in a strong positive manner—that is, perceive it as being "good" or

121

"beneficial" or "pleasant"—and then move toward or try to possess it. Love is a reasonably strong or intense attachment, involvement, or favorable prejudice between two (or more) people. It often, but not necessarily, includes sex attraction between the lovers.

The myth that there is such a thing as "real" or "true" love.

All love is true or real love in that it exists, and anything that exists is real. Love has three main vectors—frequency, intensity, and duration.

Many individuals, such as poets and novelists, have attempted to define "real" or "true" love in terms of intensity, and to contend that the only "true" love is a most intense, high-flown, once-in-a-lifetime feeling.

Many other individuals, such as clergymen, moralists, and social thinkers, have attempted to define "real" or "true" love in terms of duration, and to contend that the only "true" love is one that lasts for many years, and preferably forever.

Many psychologists have recently tried to define "true" love as one's interest in the growth and development of another person for *his* or *her* sake, rather than for one's *own* interest. So-called "true love" is rarely accepted as such when people frequently, lightly, or promiscuously love. Actually, "true" love exists only by some arbitrary definition, and all love, all emotional attachment, is actually true and real—simply because it exists. If you truly feel it, it is obviously "true" for you.

The myth that it is difficult to tell when you love.

Since love is simply a favorable bias or an emotional attachment from one person to another, it is easy to tell when you love.

You love whenever you feel, suspect, or imagine you

are definitely attached to or specially favor another person (or thing). You can also love unconsciously, without realizing that you do; but most people who love have some conscious inkling that they are favorably disposed toward another.

What is difficult to determine, in many instances, is not *that* you love, but *how much* or *in what way* you love, for there are many kinds and degrees of love. You may love sexually or non-sexually; mildly or passionately; heterosexually or homosexually; neurotically or normally; conjugally or non-conjugally; and so on. Your being passionately *in* love is usually different from your merely *loving* or *caring* for people. When you are *in* love, you usually *intensely* favor, think about, and strongly desire to be with the person you feel romantic about. Usually, you select one person at a time to be romantically in love with. You can simultaneously, however, love—or have what H.G. Wells called loving kindness—toward several people, such as your mother, father, other relatives, and close friends.

Although *how* you love may be, in itself, of little importance, it may become important if you contemplate doing something, such as marrying, because you love.

The myth that love and marriage always go together.

Marriage, in our society, is usually consummated only if you love, and presumably deeply love, your partner. In many other parts of the world, that has not been true; and, even in our own society, marriage is still largely a socioeconomic as well as a loving relationship.

In a culture like our own, therefore, you probably should normally only marry or have a living-together arrangement (LTA) with a person you love; but, conversely, you should not by any means marry *everyone* you love. You can theoretically love many people whom you meet during your lifetime; but only a few of these, in all probability, would be suitable for mating.

Moreover, if you open-eyedly want to marry a partner whom you do not particularly love, that is certainly your prerogative, and there is nothing intrinsically bad about your so doing. You *preferably* should marry, and remain married with love; but not *necessarily*.

The myth that one can be passionately in love with only one person at a time.

There now exists considerable biographical and clinical evidence that shows that it is entirely possible for you to be romantically in love with two or more members of the other or same sex at a time.

Being passionately in love with two people simultaneously often leads to complications in our culture. But the fact remains that few individuals passionately love only one person for their entire lifetime. Many are deeply in love several times during their lives and in some of these instances they passionately love two or more persons simultaneously.

Since many of us simultaneously care for or feel loving kindness toward several of our close relatives, it is hardly surprising that we are capable of doing the same with two or more nonrelatives. And since most of us tend to love that which we find lovable, it is highly unlikely that we will never find two people with lovable characteristics at the same time.

The myth that when one loves one has no sex desires for individuals whom one doesn't love.

Human sex desires are deeply rooted in biological impulses and social learning. They are often promiscuous and nondiscriminating. They are, in our culture, frequently linked to the emotion of love, but there are many, many exceptions to this rule.

Most individuals are sexually attracted to members of the other or same sex whom they love; but they are also attracted to numerous other people for whom they have little or no affection. It is therefore common for you to love one person dearly, to enjoy sex with this person, and yet to be highly attracted to one or more other people. Indeed, the male or female in our culture who is *only* sexually attracted to his or her mate and is *never* interested in any other person is behaving quite unusually, and we might almost say "abnormally."

This does not mean that a mated person has to *do* anything about his or her other sex interests; but it is almost impossible not to have *any* varietist interests, even though one dearly and steadily loves one's main partner.

The myth that one loves one's beloved all the time.

Love, even when it is deep-seated and intense, tends to be a distinctly intermittent rather than a steady, incessant feeling. This is especially true when you love for any considerable length of time.

You may steadily love your mate, in the sense that you rarely think of separating from him or her. But you may not constantly love in the sense that you think of her or him incessantly and never have any neutral or negative feelings.

Indeed, if you were truly actively in love with your mate for twenty-four hours every day in the year, you might have obsessive-compulsive behavior and not be able to function effectively in the remaining aspects of your life. You might well require psychotherapy!

The average individual who loves, however, actively, violently, passionately loves for only a relatively few minutes of each day. The rest of the time he and she tend to be rather neutral, and at times even antagonistic, to the beloved.

These, then, are some of the most prevalent myths about love in our day. They are not only widely promulgated, but are unfortunately often devoutly believed. Hardly a day passes when someone with premarital or marital difficulties does not walk into my office and present a problem that basically originates in and is sustained by one or more of these myths.

On the same day, for example, I saw a young man who was terribly disturbed because although engaged to and quite enamored of one woman, he had still been thinking sexually of other women, and a woman who was exceptionally upset because her husband, who was quite kind to her and a good sex partner, was attracted to other women as well.

Should, then, our means of mass communication be censored, and forbidden to publish myths about love that lead to so much heartache and emotional disturbance? Hell, no! But it might not be a bad idea if magazines, film producers, and radio and TV networks, which spend so many millions of dollars presenting romantic clap-trap for public consumption also spent a small part of those millions getting professional advice on how psychologically harmful is some of the material they produce.

If you would take advantage of your biological and socially-learned tendencies—and, usually strong tendencies—to love others and take real pleasure in being loved, there are several things you can do to cultivate love without throwing reason and reality to the winds.

Consider the myths about love that I describe in this chapter and see if you are victimizing yourself by holding on to them. If so, watch it!

Remember that love—and hate—are prejudices—to be sure, common and natural prejudices. You were born, as John Bowlby has shown, to love and to like being loved—else, as a tot, you might well not have survived. You were also conditioned in many ways to love—by your parents, other family members, your peers, your teachers, and by the mass media. You could not have escaped these cultural influences, which consciously and unconsciously influenced you in the past—and still may do. You also are an individual who importantly *taught yourself* to favor many people, things, events, and experiences—and to disfavor others. Again, you have distinct inborn, socially-acquired, and self-created *preferences* and *dislikes*. Wherever and however they arouse, consider them, perhaps use them, and often think about working to change them.

No matter how strong and fixed your loves and distastes are, you are a constructivist, a creator, and a re-creator. You easily habituate yourself to many habits, and you therefore "love" and continue these habits. But you still have some ability to change and *can* change your "ingrained" and prejudiced desires and distastes. However, not easily! If you strongly *want*—are definitely *determined to*—give up an old love or create a new one, you usually *can* do so: with *hard work and practice* at thinking, feeling, *and* behaving differently.

Rational emotive behavior therapy and the other cognitive behavior therapies which followed it in the 1960s show you how to increase and develop your love habits and, if you wish, how to decrease them when you want to do so, with work and practice at rethinking, refeeling, and rebehaving. You have some degree of *choice!* Not *complete* choice—for you will still be biologically and socially fallible and human. Not superhuman!

You may have a love addiction, and remain over-attached to someone (or some group of people) who are clearly not good for you—such as people who have one or two desirable traits (especially physical attractiveness) but little else that you enjoy. This is usually because you are strongly convincing yourself that you *absolutely need* your beloved's characteristics that you "naturally" *prefer*. If so, keep your preference, if you wish, but convince yourself that you do *not* need what you want. Will you die without it? No. Be completely miserable without it? Only if you rigidly *think* you will be. Love as preference, as desire, as prejudicial favoring is fine. But not as *dire need*. When the person (or the thing) you desperately love is bringing you more harm than good, give up your *need*, change it, as you can, to a strong *preference*. Let go. Only hold on to love involvements that are good for you personally. You, again, have a *choice*. Work at taking it! Determine if a person or thing that you harmfully love is worth loving in the light of your basic life goals and purposes. If not, there are fortunately several more beneficial people and things you can love. Choose!

You also have a choice—a great choice—of several different kinds of loving. You may love lightly, moderately, or "madly." You may love one person at a time or several. You may love temporarily or permanently. Because all your feelings of love are "true" or "real," you can legitimately and healthfully enjoy just about all of them. However you love, don't destructively convince yourself that it *has to be* one way—or another. If you make the most of the kind of love you actually feel and do not insist that it be more or less than it actually is, your feelings of attachment will most probably add greatly to your life. No, love doesn't exactly make the world go round and you can live happily without it. But most probably not *as* happily!

12

Sex Fascism

I began thinking about intellectual fascism and sex fascism in 1955, soon after I began to use Rational Emotive Behavior Therapy. From the start, it included the idea that people are "good" or "worthy" just because they are people—because they are human, alive, unique, and capable of enjoyment. This, as I say elsewhere in my writings and in this book, is an existential idea which I largely took from Paul Tillich's *Courage to Be*. It is an idea which you can *choose* to follow.

If, on the other hand, you choose to severely restrict your thinking, which is typical of fascism and other forms of authoritarianism, you unduly find yourself in cognitive, emotional, and behavioral chains. As I show in this chapter, intellectual fascism and sex fascism—which overlap—are narrow and bigoted systems that create anxiety, depression, and rage. Read this essay and you shall see.

Although relatively few Americans can be legitimately labeled as political or economic fascists today, probably the great majority are sex fascists. What is perhaps even more surprising is that the sex fascists tend to be almost as prevalent among the politico-economic liberal groups as they are among the social bigots and reactionaries.

Sex fascism is a major subheading under what I call intellectual fascism—which I find, among my clients and friends, to be perhaps the most pandemic and virulent psychosocial disease of our times. So before I discuss sex fascism in particular, let me briefly say something about intellectual fascism in general.

Fascism, essentially, is the arbitrary belief that individuals who possess certain "desirable" traits are intrinsically superior to those who possess certain "undesirable" characteristics. Thus, people who are white, Aryan, or Christian are often defined as being "good" or "worthwhile," and those who are Afro-American, non-Aryan, or Jewish are defined as being "inferior" or "worthless."

Intellectual fascism capriciously points to a group of human characteristics and dogmatically declares that they are "better," and that only individuals who possess this mark of distinction are truly worthwhile. The traits that are arbitrarily glorified by intellectual fascists are usually intelligence, culture, esthetic taste, achievement, success, etc. While intellectual fascists often make a great to-do about how democratic they are in hobnobbing with Afro-Americans, intermarrying with Jews, or ignoring economic class distinctions in their friendships, the attitude they take toward anyone who his "stupid," "incompetent," or "unartistic" is often one of condescension or scorn.

What intellectual fascists, in common with politico-economic fascists, find it impossible to see is that their definitions of "superiority" and "worthwhileness" are arbitrary and definitional. "But intelligence and competence," they will insist, "definitely *are* better than stupidity and incompetence. Why, then, should we not prefer a bright and capable person to a dull and incapable one?" In this insistence, they confuse several important issues.

First of all, such traits as intelligence and artistry, although good *for some purposes*, are not necessarily good *in themselves*. Thus, intelligence is fine for problem-solving and artistry is most useful in decorating a home, but high intelligence may be a handicap in driving a truck or working at a monotonous job, and artistic sensitivity may be a disadvantage to someone who works in a coal mine or is stranded in a dull community.

Second, politico-social fascists could argue with equal logic, that people's possessing blue eyes and blond hair gives them a more "esthetic" look than those with brown eyes and black hair, or that Aryans are superior to Jews because they suffer less frequently from certain diseases, such as diabetes. The fact that individuals possess some traits which are "better" or more advantageous than those possessed by others hardly makes them superior beings *generally*.

Third, a *preference* for a given characteristic should never be confused with the *intrinsic worth* of that characteristic. If I prefer twelve-toed or ivory-haired women above all others, that hardly proves that you and everyone else in the world have similar preferences. And even if the majority of us esteem twelve-toed women for, let us say, our wives or mistresses, that does not prove that ten-toed women are not good for other purposes, nor that they cannot be worthwhile to themselves.

Fourth, assuming that the possession of certain characteristics may be preferable to the person who possesses these traits as well as to others, does this mean that those who do not possess these traits are utterly worthless, criminal, and ready for the trash can? Granting that tallness, high intelligence, or physical strength may be useful for most humans, should those who are short, of average intelligence, or unmuscular be induced to commit suicide or be led to the gas chambers?

Fifth, in the final analysis, any trait that is "good" or "superior" must be satisfactory or excellent for *something*— for some purpose. And that purpose must, to some extent, always be an arbitrary prejudice or value judgment. Thus, even a trait such as good health, which almost everyone accepts as being "good," is only good for living, for leading an enjoyable life. But anyone could question the intrinsic value of life and enjoyment, and could claim that it would be better if human living ceased. Consequently, *all* human characteristics are to some extent "good" only by arbitrary definition—good for some purpose which some individual or group has stipulated as being "beneficial" or "fine."

Intellectual fascists, then, exactly like politico-economic fascists, arbitrarily define human purposes and traits as being "superior," and, in one way or another, they scorn and discriminate against those who do not possess these traits. Although they often claim to be true democrats, they are actually exceptionally authoritarian in their basic beliefs about human worth. What is more, where political fascists mainly judge others by their own arbitrary standards, consider themselves worthwhile for adhering to these standards, and deem others worthless for not possessing the "elite" traits they favor, the intellectual fascists tend to judge themselves as well as others by the perfectionist esthetic-intellectual criteria they establish, and to condemn themselves, too, when they fail to measure up to these ideals. They are thus in the unenviable position of being undemocratic and overdemanding toward everyone, including themselves.

What has all this to do with sex fascism? A great deal. For sex fascism is based on both politico-economic and intellectual fascism, and has some of the worst features of each.

First, let us consider the side of sex fascism that largely stems from the political authoritarianism of the Mussolini- and Hitler-type brands. One of the fundamental tenets of Nazism was that not only Jews and non-whites, but women as well, are second-class citizens whose main role should be to cater to males and the preservation of the race, rather than to the development of their own personalities. This is what the sexual fascist tends to also believe.

More specifically, sexual fascists firmly uphold the double standard of sex morality. They often think that women are radically different from men in their sexual desires; that they can invariably get along with less sexual activity than males; that it is not too important if they do not achieve orgasm when they have sex; that when they do climax, they should be able to do so as males do, in the course of coitus rather than in extracoital ways; that if noncoital methods of sex relations are employed, it is all right for the female to engage in fellatio but that no "real" male would ever engage in cunnilingus; that a woman should remain an absolute virgin until she is married while a male should have as many sexual adventures as possible; that it is a far greater crime for a female to have a child out of wedlock than it is for a male to father such a child; and that if a wife commits adultery it is a heinous offense against morality, while if a husband is adulterous he is following his natural human bent.

All these beliefs of sexual fascists, like those of political fascists, are arbitrary and scientifically groundless. Women are not radically different from males in their sexual desires, and when they are, they are sometimes *more* rather than *less* highly sexed than men. It is usually important that they achieve regular orgasms, and it is more important, in many instances, that they achieve their orgasms in extra-coital techniques than that the male enjoy noncoital sex play. Literally millions of women find it virtually impossible to come to climax during intercourse, while they can fairly easily do so through clitoral manipulation, cunnilingus, and other noncoital methods.

The notion that a woman should remain a virgin until marriage, and is far worse than a male if she has a child out of wedlock or commits adultery, is an antiegalitarian view that largely stems from the patriarchal customs of biblical days and has no place in a democratic society. Women, of course, are the child-bearing sex, but they obviously cannot bear children without male collaboration, and should therefore assume no more and no less responsibility for premarital or extramarital pregnancy than their paramours. To discriminate against females for their sex acts because they carry the biological burden of childbirth makes as much sense as punishing female thieves or murderers more severely than male criminals because the former, as potential or actual mothers, have greater responsibilities and presumably should therefore know better than to commit crimes.

The second major fact of sexual authoritarianism also stems almost directly from politico-economic fascist ideologies, namely, the demand for rigid conformity to a single, all-encompassing sex code for many different kinds of individuals. Politico-social fascism almost always goes in for monolithic moral codes. The grand patriarch or monarch of a tribe or nation usually decides that what is right for *him* is right for *all*, and, willy-nilly, he crams his preferences down the throats of his adherents.

So, too, sexual fascists. Either they are raised to abide

by a straight and narrow set of sex mores and laws, and, in doing so, rarely practice any other mode; or for a period of time they try various sex acts that do not conform to the code under which they were raised. Then, as age and diminished sexuality take their toll, they finally revert to rigid rules of sexual morality. In either event, they dogmatically decide that what is good enough for them is good enough for everyone—and other people damned well better agree with them or else!

This means that sexual fascists arbitrarily define other people's worth in direct proportion to the extent to which they conform to certain sex codes that are defined as "good" ones. If these other people conform to rigid codes closely, or agree with what the sex fascists *think* they should do sexually, they are accepted as "good," "moral," "worthwhile" humans; if they do not conform to these fascistic codes, they are condemned as "wicked," "immoral," or "worthless." Here again, sex fascists follow the authoritarian philosophy of measuring people's worth not in terms of the existence of their humanity, but in terms of how well they perform—or do *not* perform.

Forcing humans to conform to almost any constricted pattern of living is an authoritarian and anti-democratic procedure because the first law of human behavior is that of individual difference. Living people differ from inanimate objects in several basic ways: they have some freedom of choice or movement, some ability to reproduce themselves, and some individuality or uniqueness. When their individuality is ignored or restricted, men and women become that much less human.

In regard to their sexuality, people are also notably different. Some have enormous sex drives, some little erotic impulses. Some enjoy the same kind of sex play or coitus almost all the time, while others demand a variety of sex acts and positions for their maximum satisfaction. Some find more and more enjoyment with the same partner, while others find monogamous sex dull and boring.

One hallmark of emotional health for most people is their maintaining a good degree of flexibility and freedom from fixation in the major aspects of their lives. A few individuals may be truly happy if they always rigidly stick to one limited job or a few basic foods, but many people who are "content" to limit themselves in these ways may be compulsively or fetishistically driven to do so by conscious or unconscious fears. These people are often afraid to try to get out of their ruts—irrationally afraid that they might fail in a new job or be destroyed by novel foods. Out of their irrational fears, they surrender much of their potential life space, and taste only a minority of the pleasures and adventures of living that theoretically might be theirs.

So, again, with sex. Emotionally healthy persons want more than the limited satisfactions they happened to hit upon fairly early in their sexual development. At the same time, they are not people who compulsively have to try every possible sex variation, in and out of the books, because they can no longer enjoy former sex paths. Healthy sex partners open-mindedly and unfearingly try a variety of practices and finally end up favoring some which, through personal experience and observation, they find to be more satisfying.

The philosophy and practice of the sex fascist, however, does not permit the sex adventurousness and experimentation that is normal for most people. It attempts to force all persons into a single, invariant mold. In our own society, this one-sided brand of legally and socially allowable sex conduct has consisted of heterosexual coitus in one or two "natural" positions between a man and a woman who are formally married to each other. All other forms of sexual behavior, such as masturbation, petting, premarital intercourse, or noncoital relations between husbands and wives have been encrusted with guilt, or, as in the case of such acts as adultery and homosexuality, often have been subject to persecution.

Fascist ideologies have particularly prevailed in the areas of sex, while they have been relatively milder in many other aspects of social "misbehavior." Thus people are considered to be unmannerly or impolite if they do not follow certain rules of etiquette, such as eating or dressing in a decorous way. A person is looked upon as vice-ridden if he or she is seriously addicted to, say, smoking, drinking, gluttony, or slothfulness. But in regard to most forms of so-called impoliteness and vice, only minor criticism is leveled. In regard to sexual "vice," however, people have been savagely penalized by sex fascists—just as political fascists, when they have power, generally are against the "vices" of individualism and nonconformity to their views.

The whole philosophy of excoriating and punishing human beings for their "sins" is, in fact, a fascist attitude that stems directly from primitive patriarchism. If a patriarch, monarch, or primitive deity lays down a set of rules for behavior, and someone in his jurisdiction flouts them, he never thinks in terms of the real problem—which, simply stated, is: How can I induce this rebellious individual to desist from breaking my rules in the future? Instead, he tends to be so personally aggrieved that he only thinks in terms of: How can I severely punish that dirty so-and-so for his past and *present* impiety?

In other words, the fascist is not really interested in teaching people to avoid repeating their mistakes or to change their future behavior. She is interested not in *them* but in *herself*—in her own arbitrary beliefs and how she can force people to conform to her dogmatisms. Similarly, the sex fascist is not in the least interested, really, in what modes of sex conduct would be best for people to follow— meaning, least self-defeating and most satisfaction-producing. She is egocentrically concerned with what codes she *absolutely insists* they should follow.

In consequence, the sex fascist can only think in terms of how different from *his* recommendations are the actions of those who masturbate, fornicate in ways not traditionally accepted, and pet to orgasm. And instead of, at most, legislating against certain sex practices—such as rape or the seduction of minors—that are really harmful when perpetrated against another, he legislates against many sex acts that are matters of personal taste and that are not normally antisocial.

A third significant aspect of sexual fascism is that which stems directly from and is linked inextricably to intellectual fascism. As we previously noted, the intellectual fascist is an individual who insists that human beings are only worthwhile in relation to how well they perform—how competent, effective, and achieving they behave. The sexual fascist applies this yardstick of intrinsic human worth to sex, love, and marital relationships.

More specifically, sexual fascists view anyone—including, ironically, themselves—as worthless, valueless individuals unless they are perfectly sexually competent. In the case of a male, this means that the "worthwhile" individual has to be able to achieve an erection without any difficulty, to maintain it for a long period of time, and finally to be able to have an orgasm exactly at the same moment that his female partner has her climax. In addition the male *should* be able to become sexually aroused again shortly after he has had his initial orgasm, and be capable of several climaxes a night. He *should* be able to arouse even a sexless woman by his adept sexual foreplay, and continue to arouse her so that she has several orgasms in quick succession and "proves" him to be the greatest lover in the world.

If the sexual fascist is a woman, she supposedly *must* be aroused to a fever pitch of excitement in short order; easily has an orgasm after a brief period of intercourse; hold off her climax, if necessary, to match the moment when her male partner has his; and enjoy every conceivable kind of sex play and all kinds of noncoital techniques, especially bringing her lover to orgasm with her mouth. Such a woman is able to have many terrific orgasms per evening and is satisfied only when her lover is finally ecstatically finished with the great sex she gives him.

This fantastic view of sexual adequacy is quite unrealistic in that, like some of the other authoritarian views we have been examining, it ignores the basic facts of individual human differences. It fails to take into account that many men and women are not great sexual athletes; that lasting sexual powers differ enormously; that many sexually competent females do not have orgasms during coitus and many males are sexually rapid firers; that some individuals who are excellent lovers are not unusual responders, and that some who respond beautifully have little interest in making active love themselves.

More importantly, this perfectionistic view of sexual adequacy contains the basic fascistic assumption that if one is *not* uncommonly good at coital and noncoital sex, one is basically a nincompoop and worthless, and might just as well curl up and die. It utterly ignores the truth that no man or woman can be competent or effective in all respects, and that many "worthwhile" people have poor sex desire, technique, and capacity.

Let us consider a specific case, to examine the results of this kind of sexual fascism. A while ago I saw for psychotherapy a young man whose main occupation in life was having affairs with women. He was unusually handsome, intelligent, and financially successful, so he had no difficulty in finding one partner after another.

Whenever he described his sexual adventures to me, he invariably spoke in a highly deprecating tone about his girlfriend of the moment. This one looked fine when she was all dressed up, but she was "disgustingly titless" when she took off her clothes. That one was "absolutely beautiful, from tip to stern," but "she must have had a chunk of lead in her ass, and just lay there on the bed without even a wriggle, expecting me to do all the work." This new woman "stunk like a carload of pigs"; the one before "was so inhibited that she couldn't be oral with a lollipop"; the one before her "was so bad in bed that a board with a hole in it would have been more exciting," and so on.

With rare exceptions, this young man always described his sex partners in highly negative terms, and fumed that, since these women were coitally or extracoitally inept, they were perfectly worthless and could drop dead for all he cared. He had no interest in educating his partners so that they might become better bedmates, nor gave any thought to nonsexual traits that might somewhat redeem their sex deficiencies.

As it happened, this deprecator of young womanhood eventually met a woman who could give him cards and spades in nocturnal gymnastics and kept coming back for more. Whether lightly caressed or vigorously taken, she had no difficulty achieving one tremendous orgasm after another, and there seemed to be no sexual practices which she did not thoroughly enjoy.

After seeing this paragon of sexuality for a few weeks, my client began to notice a serious decrease in his own desires and powers. He frequently found himself unable to maintain an adequate erection to complete copulation; at other times, when he was sufficiently potent, he found coitus to be joyless and nonclimactic. He began to acutely depress himself about his incompetence and only by forcing him to face and question the innermost roots of his intellectual and sexual fascism was I able to help him overcome his anxiety and depression.

Like a typical intellectual fascist, this young man tended to define *all* human inadequacy and imperfection, including his own, as horrible and frightful. *Needing* to appear superior to others, he felt compulsively impelled to belittle the women with whom he had affairs—and who, unconsciously, he often picked just because he could eventually focus on their deficiencies and show them up. When he finally met his own sexual match, he could no more tolerate her competence than he could previously tolerate the inadequacies of his earlier lovers. For, according to his fascist-based ideology, he *had* to be best, *had* to be sexually supreme, and could not bear any real competition to his narcissism and grandiosity.

The more my client began to see that he was not sexually peerless, the more he began to hate himself for his own inadequacies; and the more he focused on how horrible it was for him to be inept, the more coitally incompetent he became. This kind of vicious neurotic circle can be broken when the afflicted individual is able to see the fundamental irrational assumptions or beliefs that underlie his behavior. In this instance, when I finally was able to induce this young man to question his fascistic, perfectionistic ideas of sexual adequacy, and to stop measuring his own and others' value as human beings in terms of his or their sexual prowess, he stopped trying to keep up with his high-sexed partner, and his potency returned. He also started to question his entire attitude toward women, and to see them much more as humans than as mere bedmates.

Until we consistently acknowledge the intrinsic value of ourselves and our fellows just because we are human, alive, and unique, politico-economic and intellectual fascism are bound to survive—and with them, their sexual fascist derivatives. Until we accept people for *being* rather than being *something*, for *doing* rather than for doing *well*, all our vaunted liberalism and democracy will be babble. At bottom, we will still be fascistic.

What can you personally do to reduce your own tendencies toward sex fascism even if you are biologically and socially inclined to its prejudiced labeling (overgeneralizing) and to creating demands about the kinds of sex acts that you and other people *absolutely should and must* have?

One unpuritanical attitude and behavior you can work at adopting is the ability to strongly wish and prefer, if you will, that you and other people be intelligent, cultured, esthetic, creative, and productive. If you think those kinds of traits are "good" ones, fine. But curb your tendencies to be an intellectual fascist by *insisting* that you and others absolutely must have these "superiorities" and that if they don't, they are "inferior persons."

At the same time that you strongly see and combat your tendencies to be fascistic intellectually, also look for any vestiges of sexually fascistic thinking, feeling, and acting that you may have. Especially combat your beliefs that women are sexually (and otherwise) inferior to men; that all people should and must follow a single, rigid code of sex conduct; that children and adolescents are to be deprived of practically all sex-love choices; and that anyone who doesn't follow an indubitably "good" and "proper" sex code is a "worthless person;" and that anyone who does not have "adequate, competent" or "successful" sex goals and achievements is an "inferior individual." You may still believe that some sex acts are often "better" and "healthier" than other kinds of sex for many people much of the time—but not that they are "better" all of the time for all people. When you or others engage in what you think is ineffective or antisocial sex, you may criticize their *behavior* but not damn their *personhood*. You may at times view yourself as having sex inclinations as being "wrong," "stupid," or "immoral" but, first of all, you don't have to indulge in your inclinations—you can almost always force yourself to refuse to act on them. Even, however, if you do engage in what you consider as "bad" acts, you can always give yourself REBT's unconditional self-acceptance (USA) and never—no, never—rate yourself globally, and inaccurately, as a *bad person*. Your having USA saves you from acting fascistically against yourself; and your achieving unconditional other-acceptance (UOA) saves you from acting as a sex fascist against others. Fascistic thoughts, feelings, and behaviors are, by definition, anti-democratic and authoritarian. Keep on guard against them!

13

A Rational and Humanistic Approach to Sex Morality

What is a rational approach to sexual morality? "Rational," according to the dictionary, means based on or derived from reasoning. More specifically, an argument is rational when it takes into account the facts of reality, is based on empirical evidence, is not merely rooted in fantasy and wishful thinking, is logically consistent with its own basic premises, and encourages results that help individuals, as well as their social groups, to achieve their chosen goals and interests. Applied to human affairs, rational does not mean rationalistic: for rationalism is the doctrine of accepting reason as the *only* or *absolute* authority in determining one's opinions or course of action, and it is the belief that reason alone is the true source of knowledge. Rationalism, because of its absolutism, can actually be—as it is, for example, in the philosophy of Ayn Rand—an irrational, dogmatic creed. Rationality, on the other hand, includes reasonableness, practicality, moderation, open-mindedness, provision for change, skepticism about supernaturalism, and lack of condemnation of individuals who have opposing views.

The main thesis of this chapter is that if sexual morality is to be rational, it had better be a subheading under the main heading of general morality. Sexual behavior is only an *aspect* of human behavior; and although it is an important aspect, it is not unique, special, and all-important. Indeed, it cannot be divorced from socializing, relating, communicating, and various other forms of human contact and collaboration. Consequently, a sex act is immoral, unethical, or irrational not merely because it is *sexual*, but because it is also in some respect nonsexually destructive or inefficient. Even rape, which by practically any code is distinctly immoral, is not wrong because it involves intercourse, but because it consists of forceful, freedom-depriving, injurious intercourse; and it is its breach of human consent rather than its sexuality that makes it immoral.

What are the main principles of humanistic ethics, from which principles of sexual ethics can be logically derived? No one seems to know for sure, since absolutist ethical ideals are hardly achievable; nor are they particularly *human*. Utopias, as recent sociological thinkers have been pointing out, are unrealistic and unattainable, because one of the main characteristics of people and their societies is that they change over the years. Nonetheless, I shall attempt to establish some general ethical postulates that I believe are rational—meaning reasonable—and humanistic today, and that are likely to have some relevance for the near, and perhaps even more distant, future.

In stating these rational rules, I shall try to abide by a principle that seems to me to be based upon empirical evidence and logical reasoning: namely, the principle of duality or plurality. Humans tend to think in monolithic, one-sided ways and search out absolute rules and certainty; however, practically every idea or answer seems to be at least two-sided, and often many-faceted. Thus, human behavior is adequately explained by both heredity and environment; personality includes cognition and behavior; sexual happiness can be had with stable and varied relationships; and people would better be concerned with here and now experience and future pain and pleasures. To understand what makes individuals tick without examining and taking into account the varied influences upon them is to have a narrow and unrealistic view of how they do and preferably could behave.

It is my thesis that a dualistic or many-sided point of view can be applied to the ticklish and still unresolved problem of human morality. It is also my thesis that although moral codes generally emphasize an individual's harming others, they usually ignore the equally important question of their defeating people's own best interests; and they often forget that people may be just as unethical in the latter as in the former case. In the following attempt at stating moral principles, I shall, therefore, include propositions that concern themselves with self-defeatism as well as social sabotage, and I shall consider a pluralistic approach to "right" and "wrong." Using this framework, I hypothesize that an ethical code that includes the following rational ideas would hardly be perfect, but it would be more practical than various other codes that have been dogmatically held over the centuries.

1. People had better strive primarily for their own welfare (usually, for continued existence and for maximum satisfaction and minimum pain); but because they live in a social group and because their satisfactions and annoyances are importantly bound up with group living, they should also refrain from unduly interfering with the welfare of others and aid social as well as personal goals. In Rational Emotive Behavior Therapy,

people had better strive for unconditional self-acceptance (USA) and unconditional other-acceptance (UOA), not either/or!

2. People had better try to live in the here and now and enthusiastically enjoy many immediate or short-range pursuits but should also keep an eye on tomorrow and give up some immediate gains for longer-range, future satisfactions.

3. A moral code preferably should be constructed on the basis of as much empirical evidence about human beings and their functioning as it is possible for the moral-makers to obtain; but such moral-makers had better realize that morality is also based on an underlying value system or set of assumptions, such as the assumptions that pleasure is "good" and pain is "bad."

4. There probably cannot ever be any absolutely correct or proper rules of morality, because people and conditions change over the years and what is "right" today may be "wrong" tomorrow. Sane ethics are relativistic and situational. However, the nature of humans and their environment is, and is likely to continue to be for some time to come, so ordered that a few moral rules will probably remain fairly stable for most groups under many circumstances. For example, "do not kill, lest you be killed," "love begets love," and "work hard to change the obnoxious conditions that you can change but gracefully lump those that you can't change," are likely to retain some degree of truth for a long time to come.

5. It is generally better for people to follow the customs and laws of their social group, the flaunting of which will bring real penalties. But to some degree they had better determine in their own minds the customs they

think are destructive and the laws they consider unjust and try to change or avoid them, even at the risk of some personal penalty.

6. There is danger in viewing any person, group, or thing as holy, sacred, all-important, or godly; and in viewing any person, group, or thing as totally villainous, demoniacal, worthless, or hellish. But many things are more valuable for certain purposes than others. For instance, freedom and justice are not necessitous; and slavery and injustice are not completely horrible, but for most of the people most of the time, freedom and justice are important, desirable conditions.

7. People had better base their morality on humanistic precepts; the nature of humans and their desires (rather than on the assumed nature of supernatural gods and their supposed desires); and fulfilling of these desires in the present, near-future, and more distant future. But people also have the power to significantly change some of their "nature," "desires," and "humanity." It is "natural" and "human," for example, for people to easily be hostile, destructive, and warlike; and a rational ethical code may therefore include, as one of its purposes, the goal of trying to teach society to be less "natural" and "human" in these respects, and more "natural" and "human" in other more collaborative respects.

8. Rational ethics include provision for modifications of virtually all moral codes, especially as environmental conditions change and perhaps the biological nature of humans change too. But the alteration of ethical postulates had better be carefully approached, with considerable fact-finding and discussion, as more harm than good may easily be wrought in the process of revision.

9. Immorality should preferably not be defined in terms of people's harming or acting unfairly toward another, but in terms of their *needlessly* or *gratuitously* injuring this other. For in the normal course of social living and consequent competition for jobs, sporting victories, sweethearts, or status, it is impossible for a person not to harm another—unless, of course, he or she is always the loser.

    Although it is easy to say that one individual is immoral when he or she "needlessly," "gratuitously," or "unfairly" injures or deprives another, it is difficult to give exact and invariant meanings to these modifying terms. Thus, "true" immorality is often most difficult to determine or measure.

10. A major concern of humanistic ethics would better be the facilitation of interpersonal relationships. As Lester Kirkendall and Curtis Avery have noted, "Whenever thought and choice regarding behavior and conduct are possible, those acts are morally good which create trust, and confidence, and a capacity among people to work together cooperatively." But people do not live by interpersonal relationships alone. Their intercommunications are an integral part of their intercommunications; and they can enjoyably relate to and become absorbed in non-human organisms and things. Ethics includes their whole range of activity and not only their relationships with others. *I-thou* relationships, as Martin Buber has pointed out, are highly desirable and uniquely human; but they arise out of and are experienced in the context of *I-It* relations. As Buber states: "In all the seriousness of truth, hear this: *It* man cannot live.... The communal life of man can no more than

man himself dispense with the world of *It*, over which the presence of the *Thou* moves like the spirit upon the face of the waters."

11. Humans are to some degree individually responsible for their actions. They have a measure of so-called free will or agency and can, at least if they work hard at thinking and acting, choose to perform or not to perform certain interpersonal and interpersonal acts. But they are also powerfully influenced by their inherited biological tendencies and their social environment; consequently, although they are partly responsible for their own behavior, they are never entirely accountable for it.

12. When people commit a wrong, mistaken, inefficient, self-defeating, or antisocial act, they may justifiably be termed wrongdoers or—more accurately—persons who have performed this or that "bad" deed. Since they are also inevitably *fallible* humans, it is an unscientific overgeneralization to say that they are evil or bad *persons*. This statement implies that they were born to be more immoral than the vast majority of other people, will inevitably continue to be wrong, deserve to be severely punished and damned as total human beings for being mistaken, and if there were some kind of life after death, should be eternally consigned to the tortures of hell for having committed misdeeds. These statements cannot be empirically validated or falsified, and there is some factual evidence that some of them are false and will lead to more harm—and more immorality—than good.

How do the general principles of humanistic morality apply to more specific rules of sex morality? Specifically what can you personally do to try to be rationally and humanistically moral in your sex behavior?

You had better strive primarily for your own sex-love satisfaction; but since you live in a social community and are going to be importantly affected by the sexual pleasures and annoyances of others, you had better also refrain from unduly interfering with the sex-love welfare of these others. This means that you had better not be dishonest with potential or actual sex partners; that you had better not take advantage of minors or incompetents; that you are immoral if you coerce unwilling individuals to have sex with you; and that it is generally wise for you to follow the sex laws of your community if these are actually enforced with harsh penalties. On the more positive side, it would be better if you fully and freely expressed your feelings to your sex-love partners; genuinely were interested in your partners' satisfactions as well as your own; sincerely tried to help partners with their general and sexual problems, including their Puritanism, sex phobias, compulsiveness, and inability to relate; and tried to help create the kind of a world in which other people were sexually alive, relatively free, and ethical.

This does *not* mean that to be sexually moral, you should necessarily go along with and bolster the prolongation of others' sex-love guilt, shame, and self-deprecation as many puritans may urge you to do. You might not, for example, "respect" a partner's virginity; or bolster his or her tendency to feel terribly hurt if first loved and then rejected. You might either decide to stay away from such partners or help depropagandize them and induce them to surrender their sex-love hang-ups, enabling them to widen their potentialities for living. In trying to sexually seduce others, you might take the same attitude as you would take in trying to influence or "seduce" another individual to change his or her conservative political, economic, or religious views and to become more liberal. Persuasion without coercion!

Also, you had better try to have sex-love in the here and now and to enthusiastically enjoy many immediate or short-range sexual pursuits; but you had also better keep an eye on tomorrow and give up some immediate sex-love gains for longer-range, future satisfactions. This means that you may often wisely give up present erotic pleasures for future gains. Thus, you may resist going to bed with an easily available partner because you might enjoy sex more thoroughly with one not so easily bedded.

Normally, it is better for you to follow the sex customs and laws of your social group when flaunting them will bring real and noxious penalties. Thus, if you are likely to be socially ostracized, fired from your job, or jailed for engaging in nonmarital sex relations, you had better seriously consider publicly refraining from such activities—no matter how silly or unjust you may consider the rules of your community to be. You might wisely work very hard, through speaking, writing, and political activity, to change the rules, but while they still exist and are being enforced, you may well decide to obey them.

Consider no sex act holy, sacred, or all-important. Sexual intercourse is hardly holy, because abstinence, masturbation, and noncoital sex relations are behaviors that are distinctly practiced and valued by many people. Marriage is not a sacrament, unless a couple thinks it is; and when it is viewed in this manner it may have great limitations, problems, and anxieties. Even love relationships are never all-important, as many individuals lead happy existences with minimal or no experience of them. Whenever, in fact, a sex, love, or marital act is sanctified, it tends to become more important than the people engaging in it; and from a humanistic standpoint, immorality, or the needless sabotaging of human satisfaction, often occurs.

On the other hand, many sex acts are more valuable for certain purposes than are other activities. Thus, sex with companionship or love may, at least in the long run, be more enjoyable than sex without affection (and an hour in bed with a new partner may be more exciting than an hour with your usual partner). Try to maximize, without unduly attempting to deify, your sexual enjoyments; and similarly try to help your partners achieve more important, rather than the all-important, satisfactions. Similarly, try to minimize sexual constraints and annoyances, without ridiculously amplifying them or damning people who are sexually frustrating.

You had better base your sex morality on humanistic views rather than on the assumed nature of supernatural gods and their supposed sexual rules; and base them on the fulfilling of your and your partners *human* desires in the present and future.

But humans also have the power to significantly change some of their sexual "nature." They can train themselves to be sexually constant in spite of their natural varietism. They can employ modern technology (such as electric vibrators, electronic music, and strobe lights) to affect their sexuality. They can use drugs, hormones, and other substances to make themselves more or less sexual. There seems to be no good reason why you should not experiment in various ways to modify your sexual desires and potentialities, as long as you can thereby increase your satisfactions without unduly surrendering or minimizing other advantages and benefits.

Don't defne your sex morality merely in terms of your not acting unfairly toward or harming another; rather define it in terms of your *needlessly* or *gratuitously* treating others harmfully. A man may harm a woman by accidentally getting her pregnant; but he may not be unethical unless he has adequate contraceptive means available and he deliberately decides not to employ them. However, since it is easy to interpret the terms "needlessly," "gratuitously," and "unfairly" sloppily, and since a sex-love partner can be exploited quite easily, you had best lean over backwards not to injure or to take advantage of your partners sexually even when at first blush it appears that you are needfully doing so.

You preferably, in your sex-love affairs, can concentrate on your interpersonal relations and have *I-Thou* relationships in some instances. But your insistence on maintaining deep interpersonal *I-Thou* relationships in all sex acts is unrealistic, impinges on the freedom of choice of the partner, and is likely to cause considerable anxiety and restrictions. Sex or sex-love relations of an *I-It* nature are ethical as long as you enter them honestly, with the full consent of your partners.

Keep in mind that though you are responsible for your sex actions and therefore had better accept the penalties that may accompany them, but you are also powerfully influenced by your inherited biological drives and the social environment in which you were reared. Consequently, although you are largely responsible for, or cause, your own sex-love mistakes and misdeeds, you are never entirely accountable for them. With considerable hard work and thinking, you can control many, but not all, of your sex ideas, desires, and acts.

When you engage in a wrong, mistaken, inefficient,

self-defeating, or antisocial sex act, you may justifiably be viewed as a wrongdoer or as a person who has acted unethically. But because you are a highly fallible human, it is an unscientific overgeneralization to say that you are an evil or bad person or a villain. You are only a mistake-maker and may tend to commit more sex and non-sex misdeeds in the present and future if you are severely condemned and cruelly punished. It would be far better if you were fully accepted as imperfect, were not totally defamed or damned, and were encouraged to become more problem-centered rather than self-centered, so that you could work at being less error-prone in the future.

What about sexual morality in regard to sexually transmitted diseases (STDs), especially those like AIDS and genital Herpes, for which we as yet have no cures? Shall we adopt special moral rules in a world where most of us are in danger of acquiring these diseases?

I would say, yes. Some STDs, especially AIDS, are so debilitating and life-threatening that unusual moral precautions had better be taken in regard to acquiring and transmitting them. I would therefore suggest that when contemplating sex with a partner and considering vaginal or anal intercourse, be ruthlessly and unashamedly honest about your past sex history. Let your partners know exactly what you have done and with what kind of people you have done it. No holding back!

Let your sex partners know your history of risky non-sexual experiences—such as blood transfusions or the use of contaminated needles—that might have put you and them in jeopardy. Be ethical to yourself and your partners by having safe sex, in the course of which you and your partner's body fluids do not interact, until you determine that neither of you has AIDS or any other serious sex disease. Be careful with promiscuous sex, especially when you are under the influence of alcohol or drugs.

If, while engaging in a steady sex relationship, and while agreeing to be monogamous, you actually have sex with other partners, be honest with your steady partner about this, and thereby give him or her the choice of whether to continue to have risky sex with you.

The general rule for all sex—and for that matter, love—relationships is to try to have them with other *consenting* and *competent* adults. But consent means direct, frank, and *honest* disclosure by yourself and by him or her. So where STDs are at risk, make sure that you are distinctly honest, that your partners are of legal age, are truly consenting, and are mentally, emotionally, and physically competent.

Sexual morality, then, when seen in terms of rationality, essentially consists of your following certain sane, sensible, and nondefeating values. You want to live a good life, including a good sex-love life. You also want to live it, almost always, within a social group. Consequently, you try to follow rules that will prevent you from foolishly harming yourself and will prevent you from senselessly and needlessly harming others. Sexual morality is a subheading under general, humanistic morality.

Though we often deny it, humans are both biologically and sociologically prone to think, emote, and act in self-helpingly *as well as* self-defeating and immoral ways in both their general and more specific sexual behavior. They are usually rational or self-aiding, but they frequently also believe, with vigor and bigotry, several major irrational ideas. For example, they often irrationally hold that they positively *must* be loved and approved by others; that they are no damned good when they perform imperfectly; that other people absolutely must act fairly to them, and that

157

they must live in a world of supreme safety and certainty instead of the real world of probability and chance.

As a result of these irrational ideas, people in our own and other cultures tend to think crookedly about themselves, about others, and about the world. They spend considerable time and energy condemning themselves and others. And they keep railing at world conditions for not being better than they are. Consequently, they often make themselves anxious, guilty, depressed, hostile, self-pitying, defensive, avoidant, and compulsive.

Sexually, people tend to be, if possible, even more irrational than they are nonsexually. They not only condemn themselves and each other for "wrongdoings," but they frequently inaccurately define what is wrong. If we were to apply our standards of sexual morality to our everyday behavior, we would probably discover that most of the sex acts that have been historically deemed to be sinful—such as masturbation, premarital intercourse, noncoital sex, and homosexual behavior—are not really unethical, because they do not needlessly harm their participants nor anyone else. But many of the conventional and legal sex activities in our culture—such as a husband's insisting that his wife satisfy him without his taking any real effort to satisfy her, and a wife's refusing to divorce a husband for whom she has no desire or affection—can often be called immoral from a rational and humanistic point of view. Let us really think about that!

14

How to Avoid Sexual Disturbance

Millions upon millions of words keep appearing on the subject of sex "deviation," "perversion," or "disturbance." Professionals and nonprofessionals keep debating whether certain forms of behavior, particularly homosexuality, can accurately receive the label of "deviation" or "abnormality." And although attitudes in this regard seem much more open and liberal than the views of so-called authorities a few decades ago, they still vary widely, and no consensus appears on the horizon.

How about my own views on the subject of sex "deviation"? As a psychotherapist and sex therapist, I have published fairly widely on this subject for almost 60 years. Some of my views, especially those originally expressed in *The American Sexual Tragedy* and *Sex and the Liberated Man*, have exerted a profound influence on professional and lay thinking and have helped spark some revolutionary developments in the field—such as the rise of gay liberation. They have also aroused enormous opposition, especially among conservative psychiatrists and psychologists, and they have received denunciation from some radical theorists who think that no deviations whatsoever exist and that sexual disturbance arises only as a fiction in the minds of clinicians who have a stake in inventing and preserving its "reality."

What about my present views? Do I think that sex deviation or disturbance truly exists? If it does, do I think that writers and clinicians can help ameliorate or cure it? Does it constitute a disgrace or a horror? Let me, after many years of research and clinical experience, answer these questions.

Defining Sexual "Deviation" or "Abnormality"

Many authorities and legislatures have tried to define sex deviation or abnormality—most of them confusingly. Some of their main contentions? That so-called deviates or perverts:

1. act peculiarly or engage in statistically abnormal pursuits;
2. flout laws or cultural rules;
3. behave unnaturally;
4. behave animalistically;
5. go against God's laws;
6. harm other humans;
7. behave neurotically or self-defeatingly.

Do any of these definitions seem plausible or legitimate? No—except, to some extent, the last two. Let us review them, to see why.

1. Although we may logically label anyone who has peculiar or unusual sex as "deviant," this seems silly, since *deviant* implies bad, wrong, or self-defeating. And *peculiar* or *unusual* merely means *different* and not necessarily *bad*. People who enormously enjoy rococo music, tick-tack-toe, rattlesnake meat, or screwing in a wheelbarrow may act

quite different from the majority of us. But they hardly defeat themselves, kill themselves, or behave badly or wrongly. What makes their idiosyncratic or statistically abnormal behavior immoral or perverted? Answer: nothing, except arbitrary *definition.*

If society wants to define eating rattlesnake meat as bad or wrong and to condemn and punish people who frequently engage in it, it can certainly do this. But wisely? Accurately? Scientifically? Unbigotedly? Hardly! In fact, if a group of vociferous anti-rattlesnake eaters got together and insisted that the government of their country ban all ingestion of rattlesnakes and damn and jail all those who indulged in it, we might well wonder about the mental health of the members of this group. Not because they disliked snake eating and not because they tried to persuade others to give it up, but because they dogmatically *insisted* that it had to bring bad results or was "bad" by definition and arbitrarily tried to *force* everyone else to refrain from eating snakes.

2. If you flout cultural laws or legal statutes, you may indeed get into some social and personal difficulties. But sometimes you may find it worth your while, in spite of these hassles. Rules and laws do not prove *always* good for *everyone* or even for most of the people most of the time. Rules and laws against masturbation and adultery, for example, have existed since time immemorial—and many wise humans have sanely and happily flouted them.

If the state in which you reside bans your eating snakes, and you happen to love their taste, you would probably defeat your own ends if you went to your local grocer and ordered a tin of rattlesnake meat or if you ordered such a tin by mail. For you then could very well get caught, and even if you considered this anti-snakeeating law the most ridiculous statute ever passed, perhaps you had better publicly adhere to it and not bring on any prosecution or persecution.

But suppose, on your own land, you happen to catch a snake and can kill it and eat it without letting anyone else know about it. Would you then defeat yourself if you did this and forever kept your mouth shut about your illegal act? Probably not. Because you generally want to remain a law-abiding citizen, you might well decide not to do this; and even if you kill a snake (which your community might still allow), you might refrain from eating it.

But if you decide to take a risk and flout what you consider a silly law against snake eating, can we legitimately call you "deviant" or "perverse?" I doubt it. You may behave abnormally, in a statistical sense—assuming that practically everyone else in your community abides by the law and refuses to eat snake meat. But the terms *deviant* and *perverse* imply more than engaging in behavior of a statistically peculiar bent. Consequently, I normally will not label you that way.

By the same token, suppose your community bans your having any kind of sex except with your legal mate, and suppose you then engage in premarital or adulterous sex relations. Even though such non-marital acts may then harm you and your partners (because of their legal banning and because they may include other harmful elements) can we still legitimately call them "deviant" or "perverse"? Only, again, because you have flouted the law of your community. But you, personally, may never get into any difficulty secretly engaging in adultery and, in fact, you may harmlessly enjoy yourself.

3. "Unnatural" sexual (or, for that matter, "unnatural" nonsexual) behavior can practically never be precisely

defined. Some people think it unnatural to eat ants and grasshoppers; others think it unnatural *not* to do so. Whatever a person does and harmlessly enjoys seems obviously natural to him or her—and, in part, to many others. Even if we could show that a sex act, such as exclusive homosexuality, is "unnatural" because it interferes with procreation and because the human race would die out if procreation ceased, we would still have to demonstrate that the human race *has* to continue to exist or not decrease and it *cannot* in any way exist if homosexuality becomes widespread or even universal. Actually, gay people could always resort to artificial insemination.

The second of these suppositions seems definitely wrong, since even if every single human engaged only in homosexual behavior, and in no heterosexuality whatever (which appears, to say the least, highly unlikely!), homosexuals who wanted to perpetuate the race could still do so by artificial insemination. The first assumption, that humans *absolutely must* procreate, is absolutist and not provable, since why *must* humans continue to perpetuate themselves? And if they decide to die out rather than to go on living, why would that decision not be an eminently human, and therefore natural, choice?

In other words, I find it difficult to think of any act that people can and do fairly consistently perform as unnatural. Whatever they do, they naturally do. Much of what they do definitely seems childish, irrational, and self-defeating— such as when they obsess themselves with a single kind of sex (including heterosexual coitus in the missionary position!) and neglect other important aspects of their lives or ruin their potential for greater enjoyment. If people want to survive for many years and if they want to experience maximum happiness and minimum pain during their life span, they'd better follow certain sensible rules of conduct. But of course, they don't *have to*, and we have considerable data showing that they often do not. Consequently, it seems natural and human for them to often sabotage what they say are their fundamental values. If so, to call any of their sexual (or nonsexual) behavior "unnatural" ("subhuman") appears inaccurate, and to label people as "deviant" or "perverse" for performing this "unnatural" behavior is highly questionable.

4. When we call a sex act "deviant," "perverted," or "abnormal" because of its "animality," that seems particularly false, for we *do* exist as animals, not gods or spirits. Moreover, most "lower" animals are rarely compulsive, exclusive, or fixated in their sex behavior, although human animals frequently are. Sex compulsions stem largely from highly cognitive, often complex views—particularly the beliefs that we *must* or can *only* engage in a special kind of sex or *must not* participate in another kind. These cognitive overgeneralizations (deification of one act and devil-ification of another act) appear notably human and rarely subhuman or animalistic. We can sometimes *train* "lower" animals, in our laboratories, to act in rigid, compulsive, neurotic sex ways. But they rarely get that way on their own!

5. As for sex deviations flouting God's laws, no one has ever defined these laws for certain—or probably ever will. If an all-powerful God truly proclaimed a sex act ungodly or against His law, how could a mere human actually flout that law? Not very easily! Since one God, Jehovah, or his apostle, St. Paul, labels one sex act "unnatural" and "ungodly"; since another God—say, Zeus—or Jesus, singles out other sex acts as "abnormal"; and since still another God, Allah, has quite different definitions, it

seems that "God's laws" of sexual deviation vary widely in accordance with the beliefs of those who subscribe to them and that they have no proven objective or general validity.

6. Sex acts that needlessly harm others—such as rape and seduction of a minor—and that frequently are against the law as well are immoral or antisocial, and we may call them that. Usually, however, we do not call a crime—such as robbery or bribery—a *deviation* or a *perversion*. So it seems strange that we put only sex offenses in this category. If you lie in a major way, especially to one of your friends, and you needlessly harm this person thereby, we can again say that you have behaved unethically or immorally. But deviantly? Perversely? Hardly! Many immoral acts, such as stealing and lying, occur so frequently that they cannot be called "deviant" by almost any normal standard, for deviance implies unusualness, deviation from a common norm. But even those immoral acts, such as rape, which is statistically uncommon compared to consenting intercourse, is not exactly "perverse."

7. If any legitimate meaning of the term *sex deviation* exists, I think we could use it as a kind of synonym for *sexual disturbance*. And even in this case, one could object on the grounds that a disturbance in other areas—such as a phobia, a nonsexual obsession, or a deep-seated feeling of worthlessness—hardly ever is called a "deviation" or a "perversion." Why, then, use the term almost exclusively about a *sex* disturbance?

Why not say, instead, that individuals who needlessly or foolishly interfere with their own survival or happiness by engaging in some sex act (such as compulsive exhibitionism) or by phobically avoiding certain acts (such as oral sex) are unusual or disturbed in that particular respect? And why not forget about pejorative terms like sex *deviation* and *perversions*?

In other words, although the use of the term *sex deviation* may have once served some purpose, I doubt whether it does today. It means different things to different people—including to different authorities. It tends to cover, quite vaguely, a multiplicity of sex behaviors—by no means all of which we can agree produce bad results. It often consists of enjoyable and harmless idiosyncrasies, rather than of truly self-harming or people-harming conduct. Even when it is harmful, as when people obsessively-compulsively engage in voyeurism and thereby sabotage much of their lives, it often is much more of a vice than a crime—like addiction to alcohol or to cigarettes.

I would tend to recommend, therefore, that we stop speaking about sex deviations, drop the nasty, pejorative connotations that almost invariably go with the use of such terms, and instead merely try to distinguish between sexual (and non-sexual) behavior that occurs in an emotionally disturbed and in a nondisturbed manner. Even then, we may have difficulty defining the term *disturbance*. But not as much as we seem to have with *deviation and perversion*.

Sexual Disturbance

How would I define the term *sexual disturbance*? Exactly the same way I would define *any* form of emotional disturbance, even though it had no sexual underpinnings or overtones. And general disturbance, as indicated in rational emotive behavior therapy and practice, usually stems from three major kinds of absolutist *musts, shoulds, oughts,* and *demands.*

Personal Demandingness

Sexually disturbed individuals most frequently make

inordinate personal demands on themselves. They begin with the *desire* or *wish* to do well and then escalate it to dogmatic, overgeneralized *insistence*, such as: "I *must* do very well, or at least moderately well, at practically all times and *must* win others' approval for performing adequately. And if I don't, I am a terrible, worthless person! Sexually, I *must* perform competently and win the approval of whatever partners I find attractive and interesting. I therefore cannot risk certain acts (such as intercourse) if I think I will do them poorly or will be condemned for performing them; I can allow myself only less risky acts (such as masturbation or peeping), at which I feel pretty sure I will perform well or about which others will not know that I perform badly."

This type of sexual perfectionism frequently results in feelings of anxiety, depression, and inadequacy; in withdrawal (including abstinence); and in participation exclusively in various acts, ranging from normal intercourse to sex with animals or corpses, which the disturbed individual arbitrarily defines as "safe," "good," or "enjoyable." Sex perfectionists tend to restrictively narrow down the many-faceted field of sex to one or a few limited aspects, because they predict that they will fail in other ways, be criticized for failing, and that failure or criticism would prove *awful* and *horrible*. Thus, the sexually disturbed male commonly says to himself, "If I attempted to have sex with attractive females, I would very likely fail to please them and they would probably despise me. That kind of failure and despising would make me a total worm!" Rather than risk the possible wormhood he has dreamed up for himself, this individual remains abstinent, lets himself have sex only with partners with whom he knows he *can* succeed or with whom he believes he doesn't *have to* succeed, or restricts himself to young children (whom, again, he feels safe with and knows he can easily "handle"). Or he may "safely" allow himself to view pornographic sex on the Internet or on videotapes.

Perfectionism, however, can also lead to various kinds of compulsion. Thus, the male who strongly feels that he would turn into a louse if he tried sex-love relations and failed may also believe that he can succeed unusually well at certain kinds of sex—such as giving women orgasms orally. He may therefore addict himself to this activity and compulsively look for one woman after another with whom to have oral relations. He doesn't so much enjoy the *sex* with these women, as he enjoys the notion that he has *proved himself* by successfully having it. In this respect, he may somewhat resemble a tycoon of industry who occupies himself most of his life making large sums of money, not because he really wants the money—he actually may keep so busy making it that he has practically no time to spend it—but because he has to prove how "brilliant" or "manly" he is by making it. Sexual disturbance, like general disturbance, usually occurs when men and women—as well as children—*overreact* (compulsively) or *underreact*.

Demandingness of Others

In addition to or instead of demanding great performances of himself, a woman can have unrealistic demands of others. Her philosophy then is, "You must treat me kindly and lovingly and help me sexually in any way I want, else you are a horrible, lousy person. I therefore will have little or nothing to do with you or with people resembling you and will devote myself to avoiding or harassing people like you and to restricting myself to sexual pursuits that I can have without you or that I direct against you."

This type of sexual demandingness results in feelings of

hostility, rage, unlovingness, and self-pity; withdrawal from certain forms of sex; and obsessive-compulsive focusing on other sex acts. Thus, a man who hates the first woman who rejects him—who happens to have dark hair and brown eyes—may thereafter allow himself only to have sex with blue-eyed blondes. He may make himself just as exclusively devoted to blondes as another male who doesn't have anything against dark-haired women but who finds himself so enormously attracted to brunettes that he therefore greatly fears failing with them—and fixates himself on blondes.

Compulsion may also stem from sex hostility. For example, a woman may hate her father, because he acted rather badly toward her during her childhood or adolescence. Because she crazily overgeneralizes and places all or many men in the same hateful category with her father, she may compulsively act sadistically toward most of her male partners.

Demandingness of the World

Like many disturbed individuals, the sexually disturbed person tends to demand inordinately that the world treat him kindly and make things easy for him. He may hold the view, "I *must* find sex acts easily and immediately enjoyable, because it remains not only hard but *too* hard for me to learn how to succeed at them. The world *has to* provide me with an easier way; else I refuse to find sex, or life itself, truly enjoyable." He also may believe, "When I finally manage to find any form of sex enjoyable, even if it is highly disadvantageous (as, for example, masochism may be), I *should not* have to retrain myself to have other sex enjoyments but will pigheadedly stick to this mode even though it defeats me in the long run."

This type of sexual demandingness results in low frustration tolerance, short-range hedonism, trying to get away with doing things the easy way, and lack of discipline. And again it may short-sightedly and self-defeatingly lead to undue sex-love restriction and failure. Thus, a man may discover, fairly early in his teens, that he can easily get to bed with unattractive or disturbed women. And even though he doesn't greatly enjoy such partners, he may take the easy way out and stick with them for decades to come. Or a woman may get involved with a highly intelligent and sexy partner who gives her a great deal of pleasure but who also makes her toe the line in certain respects. And she may upset herself so much about his "horrible" requirements, that she may acquire a lifelong phobia against other attractive and bright men and may frantically avoid all future relationships with them.

Similarly, a woman may be so hung up on the immediate gratification of having a man tell her nice things to quickly go to bed with him that she may compulsively seek that kind of quick ego thrill all her life—and may find it with other men, with unattractive males, or with some other special kind of sex partner to whom she therefore obsessively-compulsively attaches herself.

Usually, then, sexual hang-ups or disturbances stem from some kind of demandingness or commandingness— from people's not merely *wanting* or *preferring* a mode of sex-love activity but from their devoutly believing that they absolutely *must* have it, their life will be worthless without it, and they will become totally "rotten" if they cannot prove their "worth" by engaging in this "special" form of sex.

Sex disturbance, then, doesn't occur when people engage in peculiar, "unnatural," "animalistic," "ungodly," antisocial, or illegal sex acts. We'd better more accurately see it as a personality disorder that includes self-defeating and/or socially-disruptive thoughts, feelings, and behaviors. And we'd better not call it by pejorative, denigrating terms like *deviation* or *perversion*. When more accurately defined, it mainly includes sex acts performed in a compulsive, overly rigid, panic-stricken, hostile, disorganized, or overimpulsive manner.

Sex disturbances, moreover, exist not because of their sexuality but because they involve *dysfunctional* sexuality. They almost always come under the heading of general disturbances and rarely exist without some kind of rigid demandingness. No act, however unusual or bizarre, is neurotic just because of its unusualness. Its neurotic element consists of the afflicted individual's performing it in a self-sabotaging and/or socially-destructive manner. Thus, even regular intercourse can be performed quite neurotically—as, say, when people allow themselves to have it only with very short, green-eyed members of the opposite sex at three a.m. on February 29 in a public square. Sex disturbance, then, comes from a disturbed *attitude*—and rarely just from the specific kind of sex act performed.

A difficulty in defining sex disturbances arises from our inability to tell *exactly* when a sex act leads to self-destructive and socially-sabotaging behavior. The same difficulty arises in connection with love. If you fall madly in love, heterosexually or homosexually, with a most unsuitable woman and passionately devote yourself to her for many years, even though she gives you a very hard time and exploits you in many ways, we might easily label your behavior obsessive-compulsive or neurotic, and we might think it best for you to go for some sort of psychological treatment, to help you overcome this kind of "mad" love. But suppose you genuinely love this women, achieve immense pleasure from staying with her, have great sex mainly because you have such intense feeling for her, and always consider your relationship with her eminently worthwhile. Suppose, also, that you have many chances at other women—many of them brighter, more attractive, kinder, sexier, and less exploitative than she. You may still decide to stay with her and ignore all of them.

How, then, shall we diagnose you? As utterly crazy? As at least moderately neurotic? As self-defeating? Who, exactly, can say? Certainly, from an "objective" point of view, you seem to do yourself in. But subjectively—ah, quite a different story! Similarly with sex. For many years you may remain, say, a male fetishist who "madly" dotes on women wearing high-heeled shoes. You may follow them on the streets, try to have affairs with them, persuade all your partners to wear very high heels, spend a great deal of time and money seeking out and reading fetishist magazines that feature pictures of women in high heels, acquire a closetful of women's high-heeled shoes, and spend much time looking at them and masturbating while you observe them. This all would seem pretty crazy to the rest of us males who have little or no similar interests.

But would such a very consuming interest in high heels, and great degrees of arousal and satisfaction accompanying such an interest, prove you to be "crazy?" Yes—if you ruined your entire life because of this obsession. Yes—if you trained yourself to lose all sex desire when you had no access to high-heeled shoes. Yes—if you kept getting yourself arrested for molesting strange women who happened to wear very high heels.

But suppose you kept yourself only moderately obsessed with women's high heels and never got into any serious trouble because of your obsession—what then? Would we still call you disturbed or neurotic? Would we recommend treatment for you?

Let us not forget, in this connection, that innumerable people—perhaps, if we really knew the score, the great majority—have some kind of obsession or fixation. Jane Smith, for example, spends more money than she can really afford to collecting china. John Jones obsesses, for literally hours every week, with baseball batting averages. Jim and Dora Thompson devote practically all their time to building their liquor business, and even neglect their children and their friends in the process. But all these individuals thoroughly enjoy themselves and, in fact, feel miserable when something, such as an illness, interferes with their obsessive pursuits. None of them, moreover, may get in any serious trouble, regularly feel anxious or depressed, or consider himself or herself deprived. Disturbed? Yes—according to *some* standards. But how much so? And how many therapists would think that these obsessed people really need help or that getting intensive psychotherapy would be worth it for them?

Obsessive-compulsiveness, in other words, seems almost ubiquitous among humans and has its distinct advantages. It particularly appears to be a natural concomitant of much sex activity—perhaps the majority of young males in our society more or less obsess about sex, and the great majority of females of practically all ages often obsess about loving. To some degree, moreover, sex obsessiveness and compulsivity helps arousal and orgasm, because people who have difficulty in reaching the heights of sex excitement frequently resort to all kinds of sex fetishes, preoccupations, obsessions, and extreme fantasies to achieve arousal and orgasm. Millions of otherwise "normal" men and women, for example, frequently resort to intense sadomasochistic fantasies to make themselves more aroused during masturbation and interpersonal sex.

The question remains, shall we view many, some, or a few of these individuals as sexual neurotics? I would say few. For if practically all of us act neurotically and do so a good portion of the time, then the terms *neurotic* and *disturbed* tend to seem unrealistic, and perhaps we'd better avoid using them for any kind of behavior that appears so frequent. On the other hand, as I have shown in *Reason and Emotion in Psychotherapy* and my other writings, if some form of disturbance seems to exist as the human condition, and if virtually all of us often foolishly defeat ourselves and act antisocially in significant ways, perhaps we had better acknowledge this fact, stop putting ourselves down for having emotional disturbances, and devote considerable time and energy to making ourselves less disturbed.

In regard to sex, I tend to take a middle-of-the-road position. On the one hand, I believe that the *tendency* toward disturbance is ubiquitous among humans. For if we investigate the number of people who turn up with fairly serious sex disturbances—including behaviors such as compulsive exhibitionism, peeping, and sexual assault, that actually lead to their getting into overt trouble (such as arrest or institutionalization)—we find that perhaps 10 percent of our citizens have such distinct problems for part of their lives. But we could well add to this list of people who commit illegal sex acts three or four (maybe five or six) times that number who rigidly and self-defeatingly *abstain* from various kinds of sex for highly arbitrary reasons.

Take, for example, the large number of people who often engage in regular petting and intercourse but who rigidly abstain from ever trying oral-genital sex. If these individuals practiced *only* oral sex, we might say they had a sexual problem or disturbance. We might say that they had fixated themselves upon this monolithic kind of sex and had phobically refrained from all other modes. But what if they rigidly, compulsively *abstain* from oral sex— and do so without ever trying it, to see how they would or would not like it? Does not their rigidity *then* constitute a problem?

If we consider all the various sex acts that humans never try, that they studiously avoid trying, and that they feel disgusted about when they consider trying, it would appear that perhaps the great majority of them have some kind of hang-up. Does this mean that you have to try *everything* in the sex books to prove your "normality"? Not at all! If you honestly believe, after giving the matter some careful thought, that having sex with a corpse, a goose, or a knothole just doesn't seem your cup of tea and that you'd prefer to keep away from that sort of thing, fine. No reason why you *have* to try it!

The fact remains, however, that most of us seem to avoid many kinds of sex activities—not a few of which we feel revolted about even though we have had no experience with them. And even those which we do occasionally try— like oral sex—we attempt in such a half-hearted manner, and on so few occasions, that we never really give them a chance, though we "honestly" feel that we don't like them for the rest of our lives.

All of which means—what? That sex bigotry or prejudice exerts a mighty influence on most of us much of the time. And since emotional health in virtually any area— from food to sex to politics—largely consists of open-mindedness, of the ability to at least *consider* viewpoints other than our usual ones, my conclusion remains. A vast amount of sexual disturbance still exists, even though less than perhaps existed a number of decades ago. Much has changed for the better in this respect. Whereas in the old days, practically all of us were phobic about showing up at nude beaches, viewing pornography, living in a non-marital union with a member of the other or same sex, openly engaging in adulterous affairs, and participating in various other forms of unconventional sex, a sizable minority (and sometimes the majority) of us participate in some of these kinds of activities today. For example, it has been estimated that a huge number of the transactions on the internet—as many as 30 percent—involve people interested in pornography.

So our sex life has significantly changed, become more open, in some of these ways. Good! But sexual closedness, prejudice, and anxiety still are widespread, rather than the exception to the rule. The sex revolution marches on—but slowly, and with many regressions. Sex disturbance in one form or another still often exists. Less, I think, than it did before in our culture. But still widely!

Preferential and Disturbed Homosexuality

To understand whether sexual disturbance exists, or what kind of sex is "normal" or "disturbed," we might well consider fixed or exclusive homosexuality. For some years I contended that most confirmed homosexuals, both male and female, were "neurotic." I took this stand in several articles that I wrote for homosexual publications, and I repeated it in my book *Homosexuality: Its Causes and Cure*. I tried to make very clear in these writings that although we cannot accurately see homosexual *behavior* as disturbed, we cannot say the same thing about *fixed* or *exclusive* homosexuality, since that generally tends to take on a non-preferential, rigid aspect; and all sexual rigidities and exclusivities tend to have their distinctly neurotic aspects. The main reason I gave for most—not all—homosexuals' having emotional disturbances were:

176

1. Confirmed gay people in our society have had little or no heterosexual experience and *still* vigorously contend that they could not possibly enjoy such experience and must remain almost one hundred percent homosexual. This kind of prejudice and rigidity is something like racial and religious prejudice and results from serious fetishism, and, consequently, emotional disturbance.

2. Although gay people can easily have a strong preferential attachment to members of their own sex, the great majority of those I saw in the 1950s, including many who did not feel themselves disturbed, didn't have a preferential, but a highly compulsive, attachment to members of their own sex. I also found at that time, and still find today, that a good many heterosexuals are compulsively attached to having sex with the "right" other-sex partners and view even occasional homosexual fantasies as "horrible" and "awful."

I formerly found these and other reasons why gay people in the 1950s and 1960s were often disturbed. Do I still find this today? No. For as the gay-liberation movement rightly claims, some amount of the disturbance that has afflicted homosexuals in our culture has stemmed from our persecuting them, forcing them to live underground, and telling them that they shouldn't act the way they do and consequently are inadequate, worthless individuals. They have frequently bought this kind of vicious societal propaganda, and a good deal of their disturbance has resulted from agreeing with it. Consequently, I find that as we—meaning heterosexual society—take more liberal attitudes toward gay people and allow them to do what they want with their sex lives, with little interference and persecution, the happier and less disturbed homosexuals seem to feel and behave. Also, as gay liberation again points out, more homosexuals today seem to choose their way of life on a preferential, rather than on a compulsive, rigidly fixed, basis; and as I have noted above, people who preferentially choose a mode of sex behavior, even though it seems strange and different to the majority of people in their culture, may not be disturbed. They may merely behave differently but not be self-destructive or anti-social.

The question still remains, though: Do confirmed homosexuals today, even when they live in permissive environments—such as New York, San Francisco, Los Angeles, and various other parts of the world—have inherent emotional disturbances linked with their fixed homosexuality? Most authorities would tend to agree with gay liberation and answer, no, their homosexuality does not *necessarily* amount to a severe emotional problem. Homosexuals *can* choose to engage in same-sex and same-love relations preferentially, and the fact that they do so does not mean that they *have to* be disturbed in the rest of their lives.

Although this opinion would have rarely been held a few decades ago, it tends to prevail today. In consequence, the American Psychiatric Association dropped confirmed homosexuality from its previous list of mental disorders almost 30 years ago. And more and more psychotherapists, most of them heterosexual, now treat gay clients for all kinds of sexual and nonsexual problems without considering their gayness as one of these problems and without trying to convert them to heterosexuality.

The question of the basic origin of fixed homosexuality also remains controversial. I reviewed the evidence for the physiological causation of homoeroticism years ago and concluded that no clear-cut data existed to show that physical rather than psychological factors lead people into confirmed homosexual pathways.

HOW TO AVOID SEXUAL DISTURBANCE

Drs. John Mahoney and Anke Ehrhardt take a middle-of-the-road position, holding that "certain sexually dimorphic traits are laid down in the brain before birth which may facilitate the establishment of either homosexuality, bisexuality, or heterosexuality but are too strongly bivalent to be exclusive and invariant determinants of either homo- or heterosexuality or of their shared bisexual state."

My guess? That *some* confirmed homosexuals may well have a *slight* physiological predisposition to avoid heterosexual relations and devote themselves to homosexual relations—just as, I believe, most heterosexuals have a *slight* physiological predisposition favoring heterosexuality. But largely, I think, humans tend to be innately bisexual or plurisexual and can fairly easily train themselves—usually for psychological reasons—to avoid one major mode of sexuality (such as homosexuality *or* heterosexuality) and to exclusively or mainly enjoy another mode. As a result of their self-training they *feel* much more comfortable with the mode they choose, *view* it as their "natural" bent, and falsely conclude that they *had* to choose it. The more rigid they act about their main choice, the more disturbance they tend to exhibit—and their disturbance, too, has both physiological and environmental sources.

Back to the consideration of the disturbed tendencies of gay people in this society—again, much controversy exists at the present time.

Where do I stand on all this? Still pretty much on the side of sex *preference* rather than *compulsiveness* and still saying, as I said in the first edition of *The American Sexual Tragedy* a good many years ago: We'd better apply standards of emotional disturbance equally to straights and gays. Disturbance does not consist of sex leanings in themselves; and contrary to the psychoanalytic hypotheses of

179

Freud and his followers, general emotional problems rarely flow from sex problems—from castration fears or from an "Oedipus complex." On the contrary, humans who have a tendency to exaggerate the significance of things, especially of making mistakes and being criticized for these mistakes, get into sex difficulties because they think that they *have to* perform well sexually and that they *must* win the approval of others. I have seen hundreds of heterosexual men and women who have sex disabilities or inadequacies, and virtually all of them have enormous fears of failure and a dire need to feel approved and loved. Without these fears and this need they would rarely wind up with a sex problem in the first place or would fairly easily conquer it.

My philosophy almost exactly follows, as it has for many years, that of Identity House, a counseling center in New York specifically designed to serve the gay and bisexual community. Its philosophy is centered around "the ideal that one's sexual identity should be a freely chosen expression of that which is most natural to and rewarding for each individual." Well stated! If you really wanted to behave wisely in regard to sex, you would experiment during your lifetime with a variety of outlets—usually including masturbation, heterosexuality, and homosexuality—and would open-mindedly observe which ones seem most satisfying to you. You would also consider the practical advantages of these outlets—whether, for example, you have to spend much time pursuing them, how much expense they tend to require, whether they lead to responsibilities that you don't want to assume, what real health hazards (such as venereal diseases) they tend to include, and so forth.

On the basis of this information, and especially on the basis of your *own* particular tastes, you would select some main forms, or even one main form, of sexual behavior that seems to suit you, and you would probably largely stick with these for much of your life. Not that you have to!—for you could also try a particular sexual pathway, such as being gay, for a time and then decide to practically abandon it for another mode, such as being straight. Or you could mainly stick with one sexual outlet, such as masturbation, and from time to time engage in other outlets, such as homosexual, heterosexual, and other kinds of sex.

In other words, I see no single, monolithic sex route that you have to follow all or most of your life. I think that, for various biological and sociological reasons, you will probably tend to favor one route rather than another—just as, in having heterosexual intercourse, you may tend to favor one position most of the time and only now and then resort to others. Most people seem to remain this way—with food, dress styles, reading tastes, and music preferences. They largely favor one mode and only now and then take advantage of various other modalities. So I think that you will probably do this with sex, too. But you don't have to make your sex behavior—whether it is heterosexual or homosexual—into your *identity*. You don't have to identify your *total self* as a homosexual or as a heterosexual. You always have the *choice* of sometimes acting one way or another.

Before I conclude this section on the REBT approach to homosexuality, let me quote two REBT practitioners who have given much serious thought to defining and treating sexual "deviation." The first was Ian Campbell, a gay psychologist and activist at the University of Melbourne who died of AIDS. Ian showed great courage to the very end and before he died wrote a fine chapter on "The Psychology of Homosexuality" for a book, *Clinical Applications of Rational-*

Emotive Therapy, which I edited with Michael Bernard. To summarize the REBT view, he wrote:

> The fact that both homosexuals and heterosexuals tend to deny that they have bisexual capacities and the fact that heterosexuals often become homophobic and that homosexuals become heterophobic is largely because they are turning rational preferences for one form of sex into irrational fixations and compulsions. *Preferential* homosexuality and heterosexuality are healthy; *rigid, obsessive-compulsive* sexuality in both gay and straight individuals is neurotic.

A second leading practitioner of REBT who has written a summary of its position, "Acceptance and Construction: Rational Emotive Behavior Therapy and Homosexuality," is Emmett Velten, who makes many trenchant points, including this excellent analysis:

> In their positions on the question of the relative input of nature, nurture, and self into the output— sexual preference—REBT practitioners probably can be found all over the map. The question itself has nothing intrinsic to do with the practice of REBT. In REBT, clients—not therapists—choose therapy goals. A client may state that her goal is to write the "Great American Novel" and she feels inferior and depressed because she has failed—thus far—to write it. Even if the REBT practitioner thinks she is unlikely to reach her goal, the practitioner would rarely question the goal. REBT assumes it is not the failure and the frustration that lead to the client's depression and inferiority feelings; instead, it is her irrational beliefs *about* her

failure to write her novel that causes her disturbance. The REBT practitioner would help the client
to detect and dispute her irrational beliefs that produced her guilt feelings and sense of worthlessness.
After her irrational beliefs were successfully tackled
and her disturbed feelings mitigated, the client
might or might not stick with her goal of writing
the Great American Novel. It would be up to her.
The therapist would not try to dissuade her from
her goal.

How does this apply to homosexuality? If, for
example, a client trained herself as a lawyer and
identifies herself as one, and she could just as well
have trained herself as a doctor, so what? That is
irrelevant to therapy. What if she doesn't want to
remain a lawyer? If, for example, she blocks herself
from a career change, that would be a problem worthy of therapy—if the client wanted to work on it.
She might choose to work on other kinds of problems. But what if she doesn't want to remain a *lesbian*? Would a REBT practitioner help her to
become heterosexual?

As in the Great American Novel example above,
the REBT practitioner respects people's goals. The
difference between the Great American Novel
example and the lesbian example is this: most of
the culture, including most parents, relatives,
teachers, neighbors, religious authorities and legal
and mental health authorities (the latter until 25
years ago) do not call it a mental illness, a crime, or
a sin to want to write the Great American Novel.
Very rarely would one be fired from work, banished
from one's family, or attacked on the street for writ-

ing, or trying to write, the Great American Novel. Thus, because of the large amounts of pressure from many sources, even in the most developed nations, to "be heterosexual," REBT practitioners would be very sensitive here. They would inquire into what underlies the client's statement that her therapy goal is to be a lesbian no longer, whereas they would rarely do the same if she said her goal was to write the Great American Novel.

In the lesbian example, therefore, the therapist would likely first inquire into many aspects of the client's thinking. These aspects could include: Does the client want to change or does someone else want her to change? What have been her sexual and self-identity histories? What are her sexual desires and what have they been? Was she once straight? Has she had sex with men? With women? Was relating sexually with men her "cup of tea" at one time? Second, the therapist would likely point out to the client that being a lesbian is not a mental disorder, and that there are no convincing studies to suggest that any form of therapy—including "conversion" or "reparative" therapy—effectively leads homosexuals to change their sexual orientation. The therapist would explore why the person wants to change from "being" a lesbian—however she defines it—to something else. For example, is she being made to feel guilty by her parents? Does she feel that she has failed herself, her parents, or her children? Does she unconditionally accept herself *with* her lesbian behavior? If not, her motivation for wanting to change may be to feel more worthwhile as a person. Self-rating, then, would itself become the priority of therapy before the client's desire to become heterosexual could be effectively addressed. Has she decided that her present way of life is a sin? Does she want to become a mother and does she believe that it would be wrong for her, a lesbian, to have a child? Has she been living largely "in the closet" and has she now decided that it is too frightening and stressful to come out to other people and face the possibility of rejection and discrimination? Are there rumors about her at work or at school that frighten her with the possibility of rejection, job loss, assault? These, and probably other aspects of this "case" are among those a therapist would likely assess.

If, for non-neurotic and non-coerced reasons, the client still wants to move from lesbian to heterosexual, some REBT practitioners would probably demur, feeling they have no skill in that area. Others would attempt to help the client to realize her goal. That therapist might lead off by asking, just as in the case of the woman who wants to write the Great American Novel, "What stops you?" What stops most of us from writing the Great American Novel even though we would like to? In most cases, we don't even try. Second, we "cannot" in the sense of not having the talent. Our biological foundations cannot support that kind of construction, no matter how hard we try. The latter is something that we can only discover by trial and error, by effort, by trying, by experimenting. The same thing would be true of the woman who wants to "be" straight. If, as indicated above, it is a preferential goal—that is, she does not absolutely believe that she "must" change, and that it is awful and intolerable if she does not, and that she is a worthless person who can never be happy in life as a lesbian—then it is fine for her to have a go at it. If she "fails," that is, works hard at it and remains a lesbian, the REBT practitioner would help the client continue to accept herself unconditionally, and then help her focus on constructing the best possible life for herself. A core purpose of REBT is to encourage people to create meanings in their lives, to develop purposes, commitments and a philosophy of life. REBT openly and explicitly espouses a value system that promotes its criteria of mental health. These criteria include self-interest, self-direction, self-creation, commitment, involvement, flexibility, acceptance of uncertainty, scientific thinking, non-utopianism, self-responsibility for one's own emotional disturbances, long-range hedonism and skepticism. Heterosexuality, homosexuality, and bisexuality are not on the list.

Sexual sanity (like nonsexual sanity), then, largely consists of noncompulsiveness, personal experimentation, open-mindedness, choosing paths that do not entail too many practical disadvantages, and perhaps above all, accepting yourself and utterly refusing to down yourself even if you do the "wrong" thing and behave self-defeatingly. For if you do train yourself to behave and to continue behaving in a rigid, disturbed, uncreative sex-love manner, and you perceive that you keep defeating yourself by compulsively engaging in certain forms of sex and phobically abstaining from potentially harmless and enjoyable forms, you still don't have to berate yourself or damn yourself for your unfortunate behavior. Your *acts*, under these conditions, are foolish, but *you* are never a fool, louse, worm, or *rotten person*! For you are an ongoing process, an individual who, at any age, can change remarkably. And you (nor anyone) cannot accurately rate the whole of your youness, your living humanity. Try to remember that!

The Treatment of Sexual Disturbance

As I have tried to show thus far in this chapter, sexual disturbance may exist, but to call it by pejorative terms, such as *deviation* and *perversion*, and to make it completely synonymous with other kinds of more general disturbance may not be wise. Some people with extreme sex fetishes, for example, get along very well in their general lives—and they even manage to cater to these fetishes without creating for themselves serious problems. Others, like those who have extreme fears of failure, have general disturbances, and often experience them in sexual areas—as when they avoid sex completely or limit themselves only to masturbation instead of experimenting with a wider range of outlets. But again, they manage to live fairly "successfully" with their handicaps and mainly fail to achieve their potential, rather than ruin their whole lives. They manage to limit their disturbances, and sometimes they even do better in other areas—as, for example, in art or in business—because they give up much of their sex activity.

So don't think that sexual disturbance is entirely debilitating or horrible, for it often isn't. Nonetheless, it frequently has its disadvantages. For example:

1. Usually it goes with general disturbance—with feelings of anxiety, depression, hostility, or low frustration tolerance—and most people who have these kinds of disturbance hardly spend notably happy existences! Many of them, on the contrary, live in distinctly, and sometimes desperately, unhappy ways.

2. Sexual disturbance usually evolves as a *limiting* condition. Most people enjoy some variety and flexibility in their sex lives. By making themselves sexually neurotic, they tend to narrow down their potential circle of sexuality to a small sliver of the potential pie. And for few good reasons!

3. As I keep trying to show in this book, sex problems usually go with various forms of irrationality—with the three major unrealistic *musts* that humans impose on themselves, "I *absolutely must* perform well sexually!" "My sexual partners *must* thoroughly please me!" "Conditions *must not* block me and my partner from fulfilling our sexual desires!" Just stick to these demands and insistences and you needlessly block your sexual (and other) possibilities.

4. Although we have liberalized our culture in recent years so that we accept people with compulsive, obsessive, and overly fearful sexuality much more than previously, we still cruelly and unnecessarily penalize them to some degree. Thus, if you neurotically smoke, overeat, or are undisciplined at school or work, you will tend to suffer some penalties for your disturbed behavior—such as afflicting yourself with ill health or failures. But your self-imposed penalties will frequently end right there. If you give yourself sex problems—such as making yourself compulsively promiscuous—you will often be scorned and additionally penalized by your social group. So sex neurosis may bring on extra hazards that nonsexual disturbance may not.

Can you deal with and eliminate sex problems if you happen to have them? You certainly can, though not easily! For where many forms of disturbance have their intrinsic pains, and therefore provide you with a strong incentive to fight against them, the opposite tends to hold true with sex difficulties. Like other kinds of addictions, they frequently provide you with so much immediate gratification that you probably will *not* work very hard to give them up.

Take, for example, compulsive heterosexuality. Suppose you have an inordinate or obsessive interest in having sex with women (if you are a man) or in having sex with men (if you are a woman). You keep indulging in rampant heterosexuality in a disturbed manner—you spend more time than you can really afford to spend cruising the Internet and having different sex partners whenever you can possibly get them. You know that you have this problem and that you defeat yourself in several ways by indulging in it. But you also know that you derive a great deal of satisfaction from having it. In fact, some of the most enjoyable moments of your life occur when you manage to get a new partner, and some of the most boring moments seem to occur when you settle down with the same partner for any length of time. You tend to develop conjugal impotence under these conditions—you can make it sexually with virtually any partner *except* your steady one.

What to do? Can you, in such circumstances, actually change your neurotic ways and begin to enjoy sex-love relationships on a noncompulsive basis? Yes, you can. For although sex disturbances easily arise, usually "unconsciously," in the sense that you do not will to bring them on, they stem largely from self-conditioning. Consequently, you are a constructivist, who has the ability to sexually recondition yourself, if you want to take the time and trouble to do so.

Don't forget that so-called normal sex pleasures also originate in self-conditioning. As a human, you almost

always have innate and learned plurisexual tendencies—
you can be aroused and come to orgasm in several different ways. You also may have biological and social tendencies to prefer one or a few of these ways to others. If, for
example, you are a man who has trouble reaching orgasm
and who usually requires a good deal of friction to do so,
you may tend to prefer anal to vaginal intercourse, since
that will usually provide you with a "better" kind of stimulation. On the other hand, if you are a woman who "naturally" tends to come to orgasm slowly, with considerable
friction and pressure on your clitoral region, and if you
want to climax more quickly, you may "naturally" prefer
your partner to vigorously stimulate you with his fingers.

No matter what your "natural" bent is, however, you
usually can modify it significantly by thinking and stimu-
lating yourself in various ways. As I frequently say to my
clients, "Men and women obviously have an innate tendency to walk on their feet rather to swing from trees. But
if they really want to do such swinging and will practice it
long enough, most of them can teach themselves to swing
practically as well as monkeys. In fact, with ropes and
other apparatus, they can even improve on monkeys!"

We have already discussed some of the main techniques of helping yourself with such problems like sexual
inadequacy. Let me briefly generalize these techniques to
dealing with almost any kind of sex compulsion, fixation,
phobia, or other disturbance.

Antiawfulizing

If you are compulsive in your sex behavior, you may do
much awfulizing—defining your sex-compulsion as *awful,*
terrible, and *horrible.* Find *which* of your acts you define as
awful and strongly and consistently dispute or challenge
this definition. Start, usually, with your symptom itself—if

you now compulsively cruise after men or women and know you defeat yourself by doing so, you may well down yourself, or feel anxious and depressed, *about* your cruising. This means that you believe, "Compulsive cruising not only is disadvantageous and foolish, but I therefore *shouldn't* do it and *must* view it as *awful* if I do what I shouldn't!"

Dispute this irrational belief! "Where is the evidence that I *shouldn't* act compulsively?" Answer: Nowhere! I can only show that I'll find compulsive cruising disadvantageous and foolish (for several reasons). But I *should* act compulsive and foolish—if I do! However I behave, I *should* behave—no matter how idiotic that behavior may be—because I am human and fallible, and humans *do* often act compulsively and foolishly.

Dispute again: "Why is it *awful* if I compulsively cruise for women? Answer: Even if I do it forever, and defeat my own best ends indefinitely, I had better conclude that I am behaving badly, stupidly. But if I see if as *awful* for me to behave badly, then I really see it as *totally* bad, and total badness hardly exists. Moreover, I really see it as awful only because I think that I *shouldn't* act that way. And, as I've just demonstrated, I should!"

After disputing the *awfulness* or *horror* of your acting compulsively, see what you keep telling yourself to make yourself act that way—and dispute that. You probably devoutly believe something like, "If I don't win every woman I greatly want, I *can't stand* it! It is *terrible!* I *have to* get the sex gratification that I *really* desire! I am *no good* if I lose out on desirable women!" Dispute this nonsense!— "Why can't I stand missing out on desirable women? What makes it terrible if I do? How do I lose worth as a total person if I keep failing to win them?" Keep disputing until you come up with a rational philosophy, such as "I'll never like losing out with desirable women, and I'll always find this kind of loss very frustrating. But I *can* stand what I don't like and *can* find it merely obnoxious, and not *terrible*. Moreover, losing out with women never makes me a rotten person—only an individual who has lost something I want. I never have to devalue or down *myself*, even though my ability to win women may be poor."

Rational-emotive Imagery

Using rational-emotive imagery (REI), invented by Dr. Maxie C. Maultsby, Jr., and adapted by me, you can intensely imagine or fantasize yourself trying to gain the favor of attractive women, and perhaps one that you particularly like, and consistently failing. You can then let yourself feel, as you picture yourself failing, depressed and anxious. Then you can keep this same picture in your head and force yourself to feel *only* disappointed and sorry, and *not* unhealthily depressed or angry. When you have made yourself feel only healthily disappointed and sorry, see what you keep telling yourself to make yourself feel that way, such as, "Well, I certainly find it most unfortunate that this woman won't have anything to do with me, but that hardly means that *no* desirable woman won't. And even though I fail with her, my world will hardly come to an end. I can still find many other sexual and nonsexual enjoyments. Too bad!—but nothing *more* than that."

Every day, for the next month, practice this rational-emotive imagery by first fantasizing your losing out sexually, then letting yourself feel hurt and depressed, then changing your feeling to one of disappointment and regret, then noticing how you changed your philosophy about rejection to make yourself have this new, healthy negative feeling, then doing the same thing repeatedly, for two or three minutes a day. In this manner, you get yourself to *practice* feeling healthfully sorry instead of unhealthily depressed, and you *practice* thinking sane instead of crazy thoughts about rejection by a desirable woman.

Disputing Irrational Beliefs (DIBS)

You can take any one of your strong irrational beliefs that make you compulsively cruise for partners and use the DIBS (Disputing Irrational Beliefs) technique to help yourself give it up. Using DIBS, you ask yourself a series of questions about your irrational belief and write down your answers to them. For example:

Question: "What irrational belief do I want to dispute and surrender?"
Illustrative answer: I *absolutely must* keep winning every desirable woman I meet.

Question: "Is this belief true?"
Illustrative answer: No, definitely not.

Question: "Why is this belief false?"
Illustrative answer: (a) No law of the universe exists that says that I *have to* (or anyone *has to*) win every desirable partner I meet. (b) I can obviously survive if I lose out on many or most good ones. (c) I can clearly remain happy—though not *as* happy—if I keep getting refused by partners. (d) Lots of people live happily when they get rejected by desirable partners, so I can too.

Question: "Is there evidence of the truth of this belief?"
Illustrative answer: None that I can see. Considerable evidence exists that I would find it preferable or more desirable if I kept winning good partners. But that never proves that because I'd find it preferable to do so, I have to. No matter how desirable anything turns out to be, I never *must* get it.

Question: "What worst things could *actually* happen if I don't get what I think I must (or do get what I think I mustn't)?"

Illustrative answer: If I keep failing to win desirable partners, (a) I would fail to get certain favors and satisfactions, such as sex and love, from them. (b) I would receive extra inconveniences and annoyances, such as sex frustration. (c) I might never live with or marry a partner I would truly enjoy. (d) People might think me a total failure if I continued to fail in this respect. (e) Various other kinds of misfortunes and deprivations might occur. But I need not see any of these as *awful* or *horrible*. At the worst, they would remain problems and hassles—never *horrors* or *terrors*—unless I foolishly think that they absolutely must not exist and that the world will come to an end if they do.

Question: "What good things could I make happen if I don't get what I think I *absolutely must* get?"

Illustrative answer: Several good things might occur if I keep failing with desirable potential partners. (a) I could devote more time and energy to other pursuits, including working, recreation, and art. (b) I could concentrate on enjoying less desirable partners and perhaps have very fine relationships with them. (c) I could keep trying to win those I think desirable and improving my relating techniques. (d) I could gain some very interesting experiences while failing. (e) I could find it challenging and enjoyable to teach myself how to live happily with my failures. (f) I could learn to accept myself fully even though I keep performing crummily—and in that way make myself emotionally secure.

Again, you can practice this DIBS method for ten minutes a day for several weeks, until you have really come to disbelieve your irrational idea that you *have to* keep winning the approval of desirable partners.

Homework Assignments

In REBT, we almost always give activity homework assignments to help people change their self-defeating ideas. In this case, you could give yourself the homework assignment of: (1) trying at least once a week, or once every other week, to meet desirable partners; (2) deliberately trying to meet less desirable partners and relate to them; (3) deliberately failing with a partner who you feel is quite desirable; (4) for a while refusing to try to meet and win the favors of any desirable partners.

Self-Management Schedules

To encourage yourself to keep trying cognitive, emotive, or behavioral techniques, like those just listed, you can use reinforcers when you do work at them and penalties when you don't. Thus, if you do rational emotive imagery or force yourself to talk to one desirable partner at least once a week, you can reward yourself by eating a favorite food, masturbating, listening to music, or doing something else you personally find very enjoyable. And if you fail to perform the task you have set yourself, you can penalize yourself by burning a fifty-dollar bill, visiting a person you dislike, cleaning the house, or doing something else that you strongly dislike doing.

Related Problems

If you compulsively run after desirable partners or anxiously run away from them, you may act compulsively or avoidantly in other areas such as overeating, staying out too late at night, or viewing too much television. You can use rational emotive behavior methods, such as those out-lined in this book and in *A New Guide to Rational Living* and *Feeling Better, Getting Better, Staying Better*, to work against your compulsiveness and avoidance. The better you do at conquering your general problems, the better you probably will do to overcome your sex-love disturbance.

Psychotherapy

If you find that you have enormous difficulty overcom-ing any sex or love disturbance, you may find psychother-apy practical and beneficial. Naturally, I would recommend some form of cognitive behavior therapy, rather than psy-choanalytic, Gestalt, primal, or other therapies. I have used REBT quite effectively for years with sexual dysfunctioning, and many other therapists have found it most practical too. Masters and Johnson used a form of sex therapy that derives mainly from cognitive techniques and activity homework behavioral methods, and most effective sex therapists today follow their example.

In relation to other forms of sexual disturbance, includ-ing child molesting, cognitive behavior therapy seems def-initely most efficient. Effective therapy for sex problems almost always includes strong ideational *and* activity home-work components.

A final word on sexual disturbances: As Dr. Edward Sagarin pointed out, the mere fact that we wrongly penal-ize and damn sex "deviants" or "neurotics" and that we'd better stop doing this does not mean that no such thing as disturbance exists. It definitely does! And it can be highly disadvantageous and defeating. So if you have any real hang-up in this area, and if you act compulsively, rigidly, phobically, or in a disorganized fashion, face the fact that you may have a disturbance, accept yourself fully with the disturbance, and then do your best to understand it, see how you keep creating it, and minimize or eliminate it. Don't try to change yourself just because other people think you should or because they view you as a rotten person if you remain "deviant" or "disturbed." Change because it would help *you* to do so—would increase your happiness and improve your functioning. As the theory and practice of REBT states, *you* essentially largely create your own emotional malfunctioning, and this has great advantages, for *you* therefore can almost always change what you have done and keep doing. What we loosely call "conditioning" mainly consists of *self*-conditioning. And you can therefore do desirable reconditioning. Not that you have to. Not that you'll die or live utterly miserably if you don't. But just that in many instances, you'd better. For *your* own good!

15

Sex-love Adventuring and Personality Growth[1]

To define sex-love *adventuring* is not very hard, but who really knows what *personality growth* is? A great many words have been spoken and written on this subject during the last half century—in fact, the cynical say *too* many—but the results have hardly been definitive. One authority's "growth" is another authority's poison. For example, leaders of the existentialist movement in the field of psychotherapy, such as Ronald Laing and Rollo May, have stressed such personality virtues as openness, authenticity, caring, and acceptance of our basic irrationality. Those in the forefront of the feeling movement, such as Fritz Perls and William Schultz, have emphasized physical contact, sensory awareness, expression of deep feelings, and relatedness. Those on the reality therapy level, such as William Glasser and O. Hobart Mowrer, have seen personality growth largely in terms of ruthless reality-facing and self-discipline. And those in the vanguard of cognitive behavior therapy, such as Aaron T. Beck, George Kelly, Donald Meichenbaum, and myself, have noted that funda-

1. Originally presented in *The New Sexuality*, Edited by Herbert Otto. Palo Alto, Science and Behavior Books, 1972. Revised 1991, Copyright by Albert Ellis Institute.

mental personality growth rarely takes place without conscious philosophic restructuring. Quite a kettle of theories!

What, therefore, for the purpose of the present chapter, shall personality growth be deemed to be? I have already given a great deal of thought (not to mention clinical practice) to this topic and have come up with what seems to be some reasonably satisfactory answers. In several papers and books, I have outlined what I consider to be the main goals of emotional health or personality growth; and it seems to me that these are as good as those outlined by various other theoreticians, researchers, and clinicians.

The most important elements of personality growth are probably the achievement of enlightened self-interest, self-direction, tolerance, acceptance of ambiguity and uncertainty, flexibility, acceptance of reality, commitment, risk-taking, and self-acceptance. It is my thesis that just about all of these goals are aided and enhanced by sexual adventuring. By sexual adventuring, I mean a person's engaging in a good many sex-love relationships before he or she settles down to any form of monogamous mating and also, if the spirit moves him or her, continuing to engage in some further sex-love experimenting and varietism even after living together, in a one-to-one relationship, with a fairly permanent mate. However, in this day of AIDS and other sexually transmitted diseases (STDs), sexual adventuring after steady mating with one person had better be done openly and honestly, with the knowledge and consent of your steady mate.

Let me now go through the traits that I listed above as being associated with personality growth, define them more precisely, and indicate why I think each of them is unusually aided by sexual adventuring.

Enlightened self-interest
People who are well-adjusted to themselves and to the

social group with which they live are primarily devoted to existing and to being happy (that is, to gaining satisfactions and avoiding noxious, painful, or depriving conditions) and, at the same time, are also devoted to seeing that their fellow humans also survive and are reasonably happy. They are most interested in their own life and pleasure, but realize that they are not likely to be maximally creative and enjoying while needlessly stepping on others' toes and unduly restricting other people's living space. Consequently, they try to be non-harming to practically everyone, and select a relatively few individuals (because their time is limited) to actively care for, be close to, and help. But they are non-injurious to many and devoted to a few mainly because they enjoy that kind of activity and because they do not want to be unnecessarily frustrated and restricted by others and by the environment in which they reside. They do not dishonestly pretend to be purely altruistic; but are authentically and realistically self-interested *and* socially interested. They therefore think, feel, and act with considerable unconditional other-acceptance (UOA). As advocated by Alfred Adler, they integrate their enlightened self-interest with social interest.

Sex-love adventuring encourages and aids enlightened self-interest because adventuring people keep asking themselves, "What do *I* really want in regard to this relationship I am having or would like to have? I realize that my partner wants to begin or maintain this affair, but is that what *I* really desire? How much time is likely to be involved? What will I probably learn about myself and others? What alternative satisfactions could I get if I select another relationship, or even no relationship? Granted that this union may or may not work out well, what am I and my partner likely to gain and lose?"

Adventuring of any kind tends to be healthfully self-seeking. I travel, listen to music, search for interesting books to read, go to a meeting to find friends mainly because *I* am curious, venturesome, and absorption-bent. If someone will accompany me on these experiments, and especially if that someone can share my delight and converse with me about it, that is great—sometimes glorious. But I go for me *and* my companion. And sometimes I deliberately want to go alone, since that makes my outreaching still more adventurous.

In sex-love adventuring, I almost always require a partner (for the limits of masturbatory experimentation are usually quickly reached!). But I still don't know what is going to happen with and to that partner—and that's one of the main reasons why I find the relationship, as long or as short as it lasts, exciting. I do know, however, that almost anything can happen; that I and my partner are taking some real risks; that the final outcome of the affair—whether it be a one-night stand or marriage—is in doubt. I often recognize, therefore, that sex-love adventuring is one of the main remaining major explorations of life that is left to me, now that it is more difficult to pursue the kinds of physical and social risks that were available in earlier times.

I therefore decide to take my chances on having, or not having, an affair. If I decide yes, then I recognize that I am choosing to relate to another human and that even though she has voluntarily agreed to become enmeshed with me, she has her own desires, ideals, and vulnerabilities. Moreover, because she may be emotionally involved with me and her wishes may be father to her thoughts, she is likely to feel particularly exposed and subject to disappointment and disillusionment. Consequently, out of empathy and enlightened self-interest, I do not wish to needlessly mislead her.

So I lean over backwards, if I am ethical, to be honest with her; and I honor her acceptance or rejection of my offer. I may very well try to "seduce" my partner into having an affair with me. But I try to do so by showing her that it is probably for her own best interests, as well as for mine, for her to give up any phobically restrictive ideas about having affairs and to make her decision on the basis of choice and some risk-taking rather than compulsion.

Self-direction and independence

People who have a mature and growing personality assume responsibility for their own thinking and living, are able independently to work at most of their problems, and while at times *wanting* or *preferring* the cooperation and help of others, do not *need* their support to create an inner sense of worthiness. Their sexually adventuring tends to fall in a self-directed framework in several ways:

1. They rarely accept traditional and conventional sex-love views merely because they were taught them during their childhood or because they are the majority views of their culture. They intently consider, weigh, and ask for the evidence backing these sex attitudes and only kowtow to them when they have come up with some good reasons for following them.

2. They enter into relationships knowing full well that they may easily fail at them and that they have no one but themselves, really, to fall back upon in case they do fail. By being adventuresome, they give themselves plenty of practice at failing and discover that they can definitely survive mishaps.

3. They usually spend some amount of time, in between relationships, by themselves. They do not convince

themselves that they absolutely must have a date every weekend (and therefore maintain a long-term relationship with a partner whom they really don't enjoy that much), nor that they *absolutely must not* sleep alone during weekday nights. Because of their relative independence, in spite of their desire to keep having interesting and absorbing sex-love relationships, they remain distinctly selective rather than cowardly compromising in their mating choices.

4. They usually, because of their independence and selectivity, are able to pick partners on the basis more of real interest and love rather than of sheer sexuality. Knowing that they can be happy when alone, and knowing that they can afford to break off with a safe partner whom they no longer find interesting, they tend to select and to remain with those for whom they truly care and to have deeper relationships rather than affairs to which they desperately cling.

Tolerance

People with emotional stability are tolerant of the desires and behaviors of their partners, though these differ significantly from their own tastes. Even when others behave in a manner that they consider to be mistaken or unethical, they acknowledge that, because of people's essential fallibility, others have a right to be wrong. While disliking some of their partners' acts, tolerant mates do not condemn their sex-love companions as *persons* for performing unlikable acts. They tend to accept the fact that all humans are remarkably error-prone, do not unrealistically expect others to be perfect, and refrain from despising or punishing their partners even when they make fairly serious mistakes.

Sexually adventuring people tend to forgive themselves and others for having failings. They try a variety of sex-love behaviors, including some that may be considered "deviant," and consequently can understand and tolerate others' idiosyncrasies. If they are male, they may have sex-love relationships with several different women (or men), consequently to adopt a single rather than a double standard of morality, and to avoid being sexist. If they are a female, she is more likely to allow herself—and others—to have sex affairs in less restricted and less inhibited ways: to have them, for example, quickly or after knowing her partners for a period of time, with or without love, within or outside of legal marriage. Relatively few sex-love adventurers maintain the rigid, puritanical, damning codes of sex practice that have been prevalent in Western civilization for many centuries. And even in nonsexual ways, few of them tend to be as moralistic and proscriptive as sexually unadventurous individuals.

Acceptance of ambiguity and uncertainty

People who keep a growing edge to their personality tend to accept the fact that we all live in a world of probability and chance, where there do not seem to be nor probably ever will be any absolute certainties. They demand no surefire predictions about the future and realize that it is not at all horrible—indeed, it is in many ways fascinating and exciting—to live in a distinctly probabilistic, changeable environment.

The sexually adventurous male clearly does not demand that he meet some perfect woman early in his life, that he immediately get into a fine relationship with her, and that this remain intact forever. Nor does he demand that one mate be everything to him and that because he mainly likes her traits and finds it beneficial to be with her that she completely fulfill him, sexually, companionably,

205

emotionally, and otherwise. He realistically accepts the point, which Brian Boylan makes, that infidelity is a natural human desire, if not everyone's actual habit, and that giving in to this desire, in an honest and above-board manner, is not necessarily "wrong."

Just because she may be a varietist, the sexually adventurous woman is able to accept the imperfections of each of her partners; to not be frightened by their ambivalence and inconsistencies (knowing full well that she has her own); to face the fact that even the most intense loves may be ephemeral; and to be unhorrified at the thought of her losing a beloved through his moving away, becoming ill, dying, or otherwise being unavailable. Since, through accepting ambiguity and uncertainty in sex-love areas and resolving to live happily in spite of those realities, she can hardly be thrown by anything that happens to her in these aspects of her life, she generally tends to take an equally realistic attitude toward other aspects of living and to tolerate other life ambiguities.

Sexual adventurousness, moreover, almost by definition leads to maximum experiencing. Unadventurous, uncurious individuals of course exist; but in some ways live minimally. Venturesome people, on the other hand, do many more things, have a greater number of relationships, enjoy themselves *and* suffer more, and in many ways are more alive. By so doing, they tend to realize that existence is many-faceted, that everything does not fit into one neat-niched arrangement, and that practically nothing is absolutely certain. In this manner, again, they tend to accept uncertainty and to stop upsetting themselves when things do not rigidly conform to some of their preconceived notions.

Flexibility

The opposite of the need for certainty and of intolerance is flexibility. The emotionally growing individual consequently tends to be intellectually and emotively labile, to be open to change at all times, and to view the infinitely varied people, ideas, and things that exist in the world without prejudice. The disturbed person, on the other hand, tends to be exceptionally narrow, rigid, and overly constrained. Personality growth, in particular, would seem to be almost impossible to achieve if the individual is not quite open and flexible, for how can growing and remaining utterly bound be compatible?

Sex-love varietism and pluralism tend to abet human flexibility. People who think that they must only go with one member of the other sex at a time before marriage, remain absolutely faithful to their partners after marrying, and never contemplate divorce, remarriage, communal forms of marriage, or any other exceptions from strict monogamy are not likely to be marked by flexibility and open-mindedness. The chances are that, like the members of ultraconservative groups, they are going to make themselves just as uptight about general as about sexual freedom, and that their nonsexual and sexual views are going to be significantly correlated.

Similarly, there has usually been found to be a significant relationship between sexual liberalism and social-personal liberalism. Not that this is always true. Some members of the René Guyon Society, which is in some ways unusually liberal sexually and espouses full sex relations between young children, are quite conservative politically and socially. But in general, sexual adventuring is itself a form of open-mindedness that encourages other forms of flexible thinking and emoting, and that thereby enhances personality growth.

Scientific thinking

The longer I practice rational emotive behavior therapy, the more I am convinced that what is usually called emotional disturbance and interference with personality growth largely stems from an unscientific, magical way of thinking—thinking that is particularly involved with irrational, dogmatic, absolutist hypotheses such as, "My deeds are not only wrong and inefficient, but I am an *awful person* for performing them." "You absolutely must not treat me unfairly, and you are a thorough louse and should be eternally condemned for doing so!" "The world is not only a rough place in which to survive and live happily, but it is *too hard* for me to get along in, and I *can't stand* its being the way it completely *must* not be!"

If people would largely follow the scientific method of thinking in their personal lives, and would stop dogmatically *musturbating, awfulizing,* and *whining* about the many kinds of hassles and frustrations to which, as fallible humans, they are inevitably heir, they would not only minimize much of their deep-seated feelings of anxiety, depression, guilt, and hostility, but they would also give themselves leeway to discover, with lack of prejudice, what they really enjoy in life and how they can truly, as humans, grow.

Reason is indeed a limited faculty and may never quite solve all difficulties of life. But for maximum emotional functioning, people had better be fairly flexible, open, and scientific, and be able to apply scientific thinking, not only to external people and events, but also to themselves and their interpersonal relationships. Sex-love adventuring, though hardly a guarantee of rationality, abets scientific thinking in several important ways:

1. Sexual varietists, as noted above, are not dogmatic or conventional. Like scientists, they are out for discovery,

satisfying their own curiosity, and devising new solutions to old problems.

2. Sex-love adventurists are, above all, experimentists. They do not know what will occur when they leave an old love or take on a new one, but are willing to find out. Although they cannot, like the physical or social scientists, normally do a well-controlled study of their behaving first one way and then another, they often do less rigorous, less controlled studies of their own thoughts, feelings, and experiences as they sample first one affair and then another. They may not, thereby, come up with startling truths about sex and love in general; but they frequently arrive at profound truths about their *own* sex and love propensities.

3. Sexual adventurists are relatively objective and nondefensive about their and others' amorous ways because they have much first-hand information about love at their disposal, they observe larger rather than smaller samples of coupling behavior, and their latter-day knowledge serves to correct more erroneous earlier impressions.

Sex adventurers are more rational and non-magical about sex-love affairs than are those whose sex lives are more restricted, because they strive for greater human pleasure and less pain, and not for fictional, super-romantic visions of what sex and love presumably *should* be like in some hypothetical utopia. They tend to be more realistic and hard-headed empiricists than romantic visionaries.

Commitment to a large plan or goal
Emotionally healthy individuals are usually committed to some large life plan or goal—such as work, building a

family, art, science, or other interests. When they have personality growth, they tend to be vitally absorbed in some large goal outside of themselves, whether it be in the realm of people, things, or ideas. They frequently have at least one major creative interest, as well as some outstanding human involvement, which they make highly important to them and around which they structure a good portion of their lives.

At first blush, many monogamists would seem to do better, in terms of vital absorbing interests, than do sexual varietists, because they so frequently absorb themselves in finding one mate and then for thirty or more years trying to build a strong sex-love-family relationship with him or her. I think that this is one of the strongest points about monogamy, and one of the principle reasons that it has survived over the centuries. Sexual adventuring, however, is not necessarily incompatible with this kind of marriage-building goal, because, today, it is very possible for varietists to agree with their mates, when they are first settling down to a long-term relationship, that they will devote most of their time and energy to remaining attached to each other and to the children they bear and rear, but that they will also allow each other a reasonable amount of sexual adventuring on the side. In this way, they may reap the main advantages of security and novelty, and fulfill themselves best in their sex-love relations.

Sexual commitment, moreover, need hardly be to a monogamous marriage, as there are other possibilities. Thus, two or more couples could decide to live in a communal or tribal marriage and to dedicate themselves to building, on quite a long-term basis, that kind of sex-love relationship. And varietist adventuring in its own right can become a vital absorbing interest —as indicated by a well-known writer who has spent a large amount of his time arranging mate-swapping affairs for himself and his wife to participate in while, at the same time, they have reared three healthy, happy, highly creative children.

Monogamous commitment, moreover, often has its severe limitations, because it is often done on an obligatory rather than a truly voluntary basis. Thus, a man sexually and amatively devotes himself exclusively to his wife and children not because he truly enjoys doing so but because he believes, for conventional or religious reasons, that he *ought* to do so. In so doing, moreover, he frequently prevents himself from being committed to art, to science, to his work, or to something else (such as a string of intense love affairs) to which he may have been more genuinely and intensely attached had he not believed that he *had* to be absorbed only in monogamous marriage.

The question is: If people were more honest with themselves and their sex-love partners, would there be fewer obligatory absorptions in a single relationship and more voluntary absorptions in various kinds of non-monogamous or quasi-monogamous relations? I am inclined to think that there would be. And I am also inclined to think that such pluralistic affairs would be sometimes considerably more emotionally satisfying and healthy than many monogamous ones.

Commitment, while a most important part of human existence, had better be to each of the partner's individual desires *as well as* to their preferences for pairing. It is questionable whether devotion to a coupling arrangement is often very good or healthy if it is not based on the premise that each of the partners is truly self- *and* other interested and finds, because of this *double* interest, that he and she can be authentically devoted to the union. As Herbert A. Otto has noted, "The lack of commitment of self-realization, together with the lack of framework and opportunity for self-realization, are responsible for much of what is labeled as pathological or asocial behavior." For those who enjoy sexual adventuring, therefore, commitment to realizing themselves through varietism may be one of the most healthy and self-actualizing acts they can do.

Risk-taking

Emotionally sound people are able to take risks: to ask themselves what they would *really* like to do in life and then to try to do this, even though they risk defeat or failure. They try to be adventurous (though not necessarily foolhardy), are willing to chance almost anything once to see how they like it, and look forward to some breaks in their usual life routines. It is interesting to note, in this connection, that even some of the most self-actualizing and creative individuals spend so much of their time in routine, unadventurous pursuits that it takes something drastic, such as near-death from an illness, to jolt them into a new sense of vital living and a greater degree of risk-taking savoring of their existence.

Sexual adventuring almost by definition is one of the major, and I would say one of the most exciting and pleasurable, forms of risk-taking. In my own life, for example, I have found that no matter how sorry I was about the breakup of an affair or a marriage (and, contrary to silly rumors that circulate about me, I have had many affairs but only two marriages), my sorrow was always significantly reduced by the adventurous thought: "Ah! I wonder with what kind of person I shall become involved next. How great to look forward to a relationship that may well include several important experiences that I have not yet experienced!"

Venturesomeness in sex-love affairs virtually forces the individual to take important risks of defeat or failure. The security-minded individual cannot be very adventurous; and the adventure-headed individual is not often highly security-bound. Sexual varietism, moreover, often shows adventurers that they can definitely survive defeat; that they need not crack up when they are rejected; that even a host of love failures generally end up with a few outstanding successes; and that the loss of a potential or an actual beloved is indeed an *inconvenience*, but it is never truly a *horror*. This often-experienced contradiction of their foolish notions that sex failure is horrible may not necessarily generalize to adventurers' horror of other kinds of failure, but it certainly helps!

Concern and caution are wise and valuable. But humans, alas, are born as well as reared with an enormous tendency to escalate those feelings into those of *over*-concern and panic, and thereby they curtail a large portion of their potential living space. Sexual risk-taking occurs in an area where people, unless they are incredibly foolish, rarely suffer bone-breaking injury or death (as they may, of course, in highly respectable sports like skiing and race car driving!). The main thing people risk in sex-love adventuring is rejection and loss of approval. But it is precisely by taking these emotional gambles that people learn how to stop caring *too* much about what others think of them and to start unconditionally accepting themselves. If sexual adventuring can give men and women, as it often can, repeated practice in this important area of personality growth, it may render one of the most valuable aspects of their lifetime.

Self-acceptance

Above all, emotionally healthy and sane people are glad to be alive, and to fully accept themselves just because they are alive, because they are human, and because they are unique individuals. They almost always have some power and choices to enjoy themselves. If they are to assess and rate themselves sensibly, they can do so, *not* on the basis of their extrinsic achievements or their popularity with others, but on the basis of their own existence: on their propensity to think for and to make an interesting, absorbed life for themselves.

Preferably, as I have shown in my other writings, people had better *not* rate their *self*, or give their *total being* a report card, at all. Instead, they can merely rate their deeds, traits, and performances, and refuse to play any of the usual self-rating ego games. Consequently, instead of deifying themselves (evaluating themselves as better *people* than others) and instead of devil-ifying themselves (evaluating themselves as worse *people* than others), they can more modestly strive for unconditional self-acceptance (USA). Self-acceptance, which is much less noble and ego-inflated than self-esteem, exists when people decide to accept themselves because (1) they remain alive for a number of years, (2) they are able, while alive, to experience pleasure and pain, (3) they are human, and (4) they can *choose*, merely on the basis of their bias in favor of living and enjoying, to stay alive and to have a hell of a good and growing time.

People who achieve unconditional self-acceptance do so by choosing to live without any absolutes, without any rigid shoulds, oughts, musts, have-tos, and got-tos but with a whale of a lot of it-would-be-betters. They ceaselessly experiment and explore to try to discover what they truly like and dislike, and they use this knowledge for their own and others' growth and enjoyment.

Although, as Alan Watts indicates, people are not likely to experience sheer ecstasy for more than a few moments a day, they can think, feel, and act to have those moments and to make them count. They can be unashamed of their own hedonism, but can also strive for long-term and well-disciplined rather than short-range and undisciplined kinds of satisfaction.

What better than flexible sex-love adventuring helps people to strive for unconditional self-acceptance? Few endeavors, as far as I can see. In the realm of experimentally embarked-upon sex-love affairs, they are likely to find many harmless and intellectual, emotional, and physical delights. Sigmund Freud, who in spite of his overemphasis on the presumably sexual origins of emotional disturbance was something of a prude and a sexist, and who created one of the most inefficient systems of psychotherapy, was wise enough to see that the two main sources of personal stability and growth are love and work. Occasionally, maximum sex-love fulfillment can be achieved by the bright and cultured individual within a strict monogamic framework. But if we are ruthlessly honest about it, this seems to be more the exception than the rule. Consequently, if many (though not necessarily all) of us are to grow and grow, it is unlikely that we will achieve our maximum personality potential, especially in terms of our loving and being loved, in a lifetime setting of very little sexual adventurousness.

Maximum openness, tolerance, and self-acceptance, in other words, are much more likely to be achieved when people truly acknowledge all their thoughts, emotions, and physical urges and refrain from condemning themselves for *any* of them. This includes, of course, their pluralist as well as their monogamous, their ephemeral as well as their lasting, their inconstant as well as their steady sex-love inclinations and experiences. Not all sex acts, or even love relationships, are wise and good for every individual. Both sex and love can in many instances interfere with what some persons find are, for themselves, "deeper" and "better" pursuits—such as artistic and scientific endeavors or philosophic contemplations.

None of us really know what we want and what will be best for us until we widely experiment and experience. None of us know what our own potential for growth is until we take many risky by-paths of life and wrongly enter quite a number of blind alleys. Trial and *error* is often the road to maximum self-knowledge and growth; and that goes for sexuality and love as well as for many nonsexual aspects of living. Sex-love adventuring, therefore, is at least to some degree an almost necessary step to greater personal and personality advancement.

Does sexual freedom have its disadvantages and limitations? Of course it does! In an essay on "Group Marriage: A Possible Alternative?," I point out that this form of varietist relating is "a logical alternative to monogamous and to other forms of marriage for a select few." In one of my most controversial books, *The Civilized Couple's Guide to Extra-Marital Adventure*, I show that what I call "civilized adultery" (that is, honest adultery engaged in with the consent of one's marital partner) is highly beneficial to some individuals, but that there are as yet not too many couples who can undisturbedly accept it. All new and less limiting forms of mating tend to be difficult for people, especially those reared in our society, to follow, and require a good deal of emotional stability and intellectual wisdom on the part of those who attempt to engage in these unusual sex-love modes.

Herbert Otto, in commenting on my somewhat cautious approach to group marriage, notes that "jealousy and interpersonal conflict in the group are some of the main reasons why Ellis believes group marriage faces great difficulties. [But] group dynamic techniques, or the encounter group approach, with the help of competent professionals, might go a long way toward resolving some of the problems inherent in a group marriage structure."

I agree with Otto that efficient group (and individual) therapy can help couples be saner and happier in both regular and less regular forms of mating, and have specifically shown how rational emotive behavior therapy (REBT) can help people remain rationally jealous but surrender their irrational, insecurity-based jealousy. But I still hold that humans are exceptionally human. They are and probably always will remain very fallible. They tend to be enormously different from each other and variable in their own doings. Practically all kinds of sex-love relations, moreover, have their intrinsic difficulties and their unideal aspects. Even the healthiest personalities, consequently, are going to have to work their way through various kinds of sexual arrangements until they individually find what is better for themselves. Perhaps this is not an inevitable fact of life, but it certainly seems to be one that is highly probable.

Because of the above-mentioned human fallibilities and widespread individual differences, personal experimentation and risk-taking in sex-love affairs is still often desirable. Sex-love adventuring, as noted in this chapter, gives maximum leeway for this kind of experimentation. I therefore contend that it is one of the sanest and most enlightened paths to sex, love, marital, and personal growth.

16

The Right to Sexual Enjoyment

The time has come to recapitulate some of the main points that have been made in this book.

If I were, in a single sentence, to summarize the gist of what I have been saying, that sentence would read something like this: All people, just because they exist, should have the right to as much (or as little), as varied (or as monotonous), as intense (or as mild), as enduring (or as brief) sex enjoyments as they prefer—as long as, in the process of acquiring these preferred satisfactions, they do not needlessly, forcefully, or unfairly interfere with the sexual (or non-sexual) rights and satisfactions of others.

This means, more specifically, that in my views society should not legislate or invoke sanctions against sex acts performed by individuals who are reasonably competent and well-educated adults; who use no force or duress in the course of having sex; who do not, without the consent of their partners, specifically injure these partners; and who participate in their sex activities privately, out of sight and sound of unwilling observers.

If this and only this restriction were applied today, few

sex acts would be immoral and illegal. Included among these antisocial activities would be seduction of a minor by an adult; rape; sexual assault and murder; and exploitative dishonesty with partners.

Assuming that only these types of sex acts should be banned, are there any other kinds which should be permissible, and yet which individuals should personally avoid? Yes, I think there are.

Rational, self-helping people should normally refrain from engaging in any form of sex that is self-defeating or self-injurious. More concretely: they preferably should avoid sex that (a) leads to physical injury (e.g., extreme sexual masochism); (b) is psychologically constricting or maiming (e.g., being a too passive and dependent partner in a straight or gay relationship); (c) is distinctly unsatisfactory or uninteresting (e.g., exclusive and phobic resort to masturbating when other more enjoyable kinds of sex are available); (d) is largely motivated by anxiety, hostility, or other neurotic feelings rather than by honest preference (e.g., compulsive peeping used as a substitute for dating); or (e) interferes with nonsexual desires which may be more important than sexual gratifications (e.g., having an adulterous affair that could easily ruin one's happy marital and family life).

In actual practice (alas!), our own society has sex laws and mores that force most highly sexed individuals to curb the overwhelming majority of their sex desires and interests.

Even if people choose to remain unmated all their lives, and thus to avoid complicating alliances, they must, if they are to remain out of trouble, avoid affairs with willing married partners, petting in public, wearing "too sexy" clothing, purchasing some kinds of pornography, etc.

Quite aside from these legal restrictions, normal members of our culture will curb their sex inclinations so that they do not too seriously offend the sensibilities of their relatives, friends, lovers, neighbors, and employers. If they do not exert distinct control, they will often find themselves in social and economic difficulties and do themselves much harm and little good.

If what has just been said is accurate, it should be apparent that the average, and particularly the highly sexed, people in our culture are, sexually speaking, in a pretty kettle of paradoxes.

On the one hand, they theoretically have the right to engage in any preferential sex acts that are not injurious to others—which seems to leave them wide latitude. But, on the other hand, if they are wise enough to abide by these sex rights, they may be foolish enough to perform several actions which, because of society's antisexual attitudes, may lead to sorry consequences. What, under the circumstances, can the poor devils do?

The first thing people can do is to reduce the unnecessary or superfluous restrictions which society seems to be imposing on them but which, in the last analysis, they actually impose on themselves. Granted that it would be wrong for them literally to force themselves on others or harm them sexually. Granted, also, that it would be to engage in sex acts, such as intercourse with a fully developed but technically underage girl or boy for which they are likely to be legally penalized.

The fact remains, however, that there are a good many other sex acts that, although socially disapproved in our culture, *actually* carry no penalty but verbal disapproval. And if you can inure yourself—as you *can*—against being affected by verbal condemnation of what you honestly consider to be your own perfectly harmless sex behavior, you can largely disarm others' carping and render their censure void.

Take, for example, masturbation, petting, and premarital coitus. All these activities are highly disapproved by millions of people in our society. And other millions, in consequence, refrain from engaging in them, or else participate with considerable guilt.

If, however, you personally do not *want* to refrain from or to be guilty about masturbation, petting to orgasm, or prenuptial affairs, there is no reason why you *need* to refrain or be guilty. For these are the kind of activities that today, *only* result in verbal censure but rarely lead to specific other penalties.

Thus, even if your relatives, friends, and business associates know full well, in present-day America, that you pet or fornicate it is most unlikely that they will throw you out of your house, cut you dead in the street, or fire you from your job. Occasionally, if they are sufficiently disturbed, they might invoke such real penalties; but this would be rare. Mostly, they would merely *think* and *talk* their disapproval.

You therefore have two good possibilities in dealing with people who disagree with your harmless sex activities: (1) discreetly refrain from letting them know about these activities; or (2) let them know full well what your sex life is, but not give a fig when they disapprove.

Usually, social disapproval is only hurtful in direct proportion to your *own* vulnerability to it. If you would, after due consideration, have the courage to disagree with what others think of your sex behavior, and *not to take their criticism seriously*, you would not make yourself upset about sexual condemnation—except, as we noted before, when this condemnation is backed by legal or socio-economic penalties. Fortunately, it often isn't.

You can also write, speak, draw, sing, choreograph, and generally use all kinds of communication to proclaim against the silly social disapproval that still exists about harmless, satisfying, voluntarily performed sex acts.

If a sufficient number of Americans believe, as I do, that truly harmful and antisocial sex behavior should be curbed, but that other sex acts should be, if anything, encouraged; and if enough of these sexual democrats openly say, by their words and deeds, what they believe, our anti-sexual codes will more quickly and profoundly wither away.

This has been the fond hope of Sol Gordon, who for the last half century has crusaded in many talks, articles, and books for liberalizing our sex attitudes and laws. In books like *The Sexual Adolescent*, he has taken the courageous view that teenagers, too, are able to be told the hard facts of human sexuality, including its harmless pleasures (e.g., masturbation and petting) and its real dangers (e.g., pregnancy and venereal disease) and can be sensibly told how to avoid the latter and enjoy the former. Sol, at great risk to himself, has consistently advocated beneficial sex for children.

As early as 1974, however, Sol Gordon realized that the Christian right and other conservative sex censors in the United States and, by their strongly advocating complete abstinence (including no petting) and by their banning contraception information in the schools were promoting "millions of unintended pregnancies among girls between 11 and 17."

Despite immense opposition to and censorship of his own pro-sexual views, Sol has continued to promote them to this day. Recently, he has been joined by Judith Levine, a remarkably effective journalist and author, who has written *Harmful to Minors: The Perils of Protecting Children From Sex*. Like Gordon, Levine has most courageously documented and promulgated the heretical thesis that our children are to be *saved* from moralistic sex persecution and censorship and *saved* from abstinence-based sex education and statutory rape laws so that they can be allowed to lead harmless and healthy sex lives. To say the least, Gordon and Levine provide us with a distinctly minority view of how good sex is for children and adolescents. Fortunately, however, this unusual minority has been joined by a number of other authorities, such as Dr. Jocelyn M. Elders, a professor emeritus of pediatric endocrinology and a former Surgeon General of the U.S. Public Health Service, who wrote a favorable foreword to *Harmful to Minors*.

Frankly, I had never heard of Judith Levine until Sol Gordon recently sent me a copy of her book. Now I shall never forget her. She beautifully and thoroughly documents a main finding of this revised edition of *Sex Without Guilt*. As I and many other sex liberals have long acknowledged, today's attitudes are in many ways less puritanical than when I wrote the first edition of the book more than 40 years ago. Witness, as just a few examples, explicit sex in regular and cable television movies; openly sexual communications that flood the internet; widespread sale of pornographic books and videotapes; the free use of four-letter words in public talks, in books, and in movies, and almost everywhere else. How different from in 1958!

Personally, I think this is great, and as I said before in this book, I am happy that I had the courage, starting in the 1940s, to pioneeringly encourage some of this sex liberalism in public and professional circles. I was roundly criticized at that time for being so sexually open, but I survived!

Read, however, Judith Levine's book, and you will readily see how sexually inhibited, restricted, and censured we still are and how far off real sex freedom is. The puritanical restrictions that Sol Gordon showed to be incipient back in 1974 have now become actual with a vengeance. And not just for teenagers—for practically *all* of us. If not completely crassly, then at the very least, subtly and unconsciously.

As a result of our cultural sex repression—and similar sex suppression in most cultures of the world—who of us, in the beginning of the 21st century, is thoroughly free to talk and write about our masturbating, petting to orgasm, having premarital intercourse, engaging in adventurous affairs, having incestuous fantasies, patronizing prostitutes, fantasizing having sex with animals, and with teenagers, etc.? Damned few!

All of these forbidden and squelched activities, however, and especially those we merely fantasize about, can under some conditions be harmless to ourselves and to our fantasized partners. For example, I can harmlessly imagine myself having consenting sex with my mother, my sister, and ten thousand virgins. As long as I do not spend too much time indulging in these "wrong" fantasies, who—including myself and my fantasized partners—am I really harming? If I am constantly obsessed with these sexual fantasies, I am acting in a fruitless, disturbed manner that will distract me from other important aspects of my life. So I'd better watch my disturbance and use rational emotive behavior therapy—or some other form of effective therapy—to let me keep my fantasies while not insisting that they *have to* work out in reality, and through my unrealistic *demands* about them, make myself obsessed with them.

Before I conclude this book, let me quote somewhat from The Declaration of Sexual Rights adopted by the World Association of Sexology in Valencia, Spain in 1997 and revised on August 26, 1999. Since that time it has been promulgated in many world media. It includes eleven major points, but I shall only quote the first five:

Sexual health is the result of an environment that recognizes, respects, and exercises these sexual rights:

1. The right to sexual freedom. Sexual freedom encompasses the possibility for individuals to express their full sexual potential. However, this excludes all form of sexual coercion, exploitation and abuse at any time and situations in life.

2. The right to sexual autonomy, sexual integrity, and safety of the sexual body. This right involves the ability to make autonomous decisions about one's sexual life within a context of one's own personal and social ethics. It also encompasses control and enjoyment of our own bodies free from torture, mutilation and violence of any sort.

3. The right to sexual privacy. This involves the right for individual decisions and behaviors about intimacy as long as they do not intrude on the sexual rights of others.

4. The right to sexual equity. This refers to freedom from all forms of discrimination regardless of sex, gender, sexual orientation, age, race, social class, religion, or physical and emotional disability.

5. The right to sexual pleasure. Sexual pleasure, including autoeroticism, is a source of physical, psychological, intellectual and spiritual well-being.

As I think you can see, these sexual rights are extremely similar to those that I subscribe to in this book. I did so in the first edition of *Sex Without Guilt*; and I still do!

To repeat and to conclude. By all means refrain from sex that needlessly, forcefully, or unfairly harm others; and, to remain rational, ethical, and emotionally undisturbed, don't engage in sex that is directly self-defeating or that deprives you of the time and energy that you could use to creatively enjoy more fulfilling nonsexual interests and involvements.

Choose to set your own limits. Nevertheless!—you have the human right to engage in many sex-love relations of your individual tastes, preferences, inclinations, and urges. The more you speak up and fight for that right, and to help your partners and other people to speak up and fight for their sex-love rights, the more you are likely to realize and enjoy them. What are you waiting for?

Selected References

Most of the references to the first edition of this book are outdated, so only a few have been included in the following list. Many up to date references have been added, especially some modern sex manuals. Several recent new books on Rational Emotive Behavior Therapy (REBT) are also included in this list. Most of these books and many other materials on REBT are listed in the regular free catalogue of the Albert Ellis Institute, 45 East 65th Street, New York, NY 10021 and may be obtained by writing to the Institute and sending your mailing address.

Barash, D.L., & Lipton, J.E. *The myth of monogamy: Fidelity and infidelity in animals and people.* New York: Freeman, 2001.

Bass, B.A. Behavior therapy and the radicalization of male sexuality. *Behavior Therapist*, October, 167-168, 2002.

Bowlby, J. *Attachment and loss.* New York: Basic Books, 1969.

Comfort, A. *Sexual behavior in society.* London: Duckworth, 1950.

Comfort, A. *The joy of sex. Fully revised and completely updated for the 21st century.* New York: Crown Publishers, 2002.

Corn, L. *52 Invitations to great sex*. Santa Monica, CA: Park Avenue Publishers, 1999.

Dodson, B. *Sex for one*. New York: Author, 2001.

Dodson, B. *Orgasms for two*. New York: Harmony Books, 2002.

Dryden, W. (Ed). *Idiosyncratic rational emotive behavior therapy*. Ross-on-Rye, England: Pees, 2002.

Editors of Penthouse Magazine *26 Nights: A sexual adventure*. New York: Warner books, 2001.

Ellis, A. *The folklore of sex*. Rev. ed. New York: Grove Press, 1951.

Ellis, A. *Sex Life of the American Woman and the Kinsey Report*. New York: Greenberg, 1953.

Ellis, A. *The psychology of sex offenders*. Springfield, IL: Thomas, 1956.

Ellis, A. *Sex without guilt*. North Hollywood, CA: Wilshire Books, 1958/1965.

Ellis, A. *The art and science of love*. New York: Lyle Stuart, 1960.

Ellis, A. *The American sexual tragedy*. Rev. ed. New York: Lyle Stuart and Grove Press, 1962.

Ellis, A. *Reason and emotion in psychotherapy*. Secaucus, NJ: Citadel Press, 1962.

Ellis, A. *If this be sexual heresy*. New York: Lyle Stuart, 1963.

Ellis, A. *The intelligent woman's guide to manhunting*. New York: Lyle Stuart and Dell Publishing. Rev. ed.: *The intelligent woman's guide to dating and mating*. Secaucus, NJ: Lyle Stuart, 1979.

Ellis, A. *Sex and the single man*. New York: Lyle Stuart, 1963.

Ellis, A. *The case for sexual liberty*. Tucson, AZ: Seymour Press, 1965a.

Ellis, A. *Homosexuality: Its causes and cure*. New York: Lyle Stuart, 1965b.

Ellis, A. *Suppressed: Seven key essays publishers dared not print.* Chicago: New Classics House, 1965c.

Ellis, A. *The civilized couple's guide to extramarital adventure.* New York: Pinnacle Books, 1972.

Ellis, A. *Psychotherapy and the value of a human being.* New York: Albert Ellis Institute, 1972/1991.

Ellis, A. (speaker). *How to stubbornly refuse to be ashamed of anything.* Cassette recording. New York: Albert Ellis Institute, 1973.

Ellis, A. The rational-emotive approach to sex therapy. *Counseling Psychologist,* 5(1), 14-22, 1975.

Ellis, A. The biological basis of human irrationality. *Journal of Individual Psychology,* 32, 145-168. Reprinted: New York: Albert Ellis Institute, 1976.

Ellis, A. RET abolishes most of the human ego. *Psychotherapy,* 13, 343-348. Reprinted: New York: The Abert Ellis Institute. 1976, Rev. ed., 1991.

Ellis, A. *Sex and the liberated man.* Secaucus, NJ: Lyle Stuart Inc., 1976.

Ellis, A. *How to stubbornly refuse to make yourself miserable about anything—yes, anything!* New York: Kensington Publishers, 1988.

Ellis, A. How I became interested in sexology and sex therapy. In B. Bullough, V.L. Bullough, M.A. Fithian, W.E. Hartman, & R.S. Klein (Eds.), *Personal stories of "How I Got Into Sex"* (pp. 131-140). Amherst, NY: Prometheus Books, 1997.

Ellis, A. *How to make yourself happy and remarkably less disturbable.* Atascadero, CA: Impact Publishers, 1999.

Ellis, A. *How to control your anxiety before it controls you.* New York: Citadel Press, 2000a.

Ellis, A. Rational Emotive Imagery. In M.E. Bernard & J.L. Wolfe (Eds.), *The REBT resource book for practitioners* (2nd ed.). New York: Albert Ellis Institute, 2000.

Ellis, A. *Feeling better, getting better, and staying better.* Atascadero, CA: Impact Publishers, 2001a.

Ellis, A. *Overcoming destructive beliefs, feelings, and behaviors.* Amherst, NY: Prometheus, 2001b.

Ellis, A. *Anger: How to live with and without it.* Rev. ed. New York: Citadel Press, 2003.

Ellis, A., & Abarbanel, A. (Eds.). *Encyclopedia of sexual behavior.* New York: Hawthorne, 1960.

Ellis, A., & Bernard, M. (Eds.). *Clinical applications of rational emotive therapy.* New York: Plenum, 1985.

Ellis, A., & Blau, S. (Eds.). *The Albert Ellis reader.* New York: Kensington Publishers, 1998.

Ellis, A., & Brancale, R. *The psychology of sex offenders.* Springfield, IL: Charles Thomas, 1956.

Ellis, A., & Crawford, T. *Making intimate connections.* Atascadero, CA: Impact Publishers, 2000.

Ellis, A., & Dryden, W. Transcript of demonstration session. Commentary on Albert Ellis's demonstration session by Windy Dryden and Albert Ellis. In W. Dryden, *Practical skills in rational emotive behavior therapy* (pp. 91-117). London: Whurr, 1996.

Ellis, A., & Dryden, W. *The practice of rational emotive behavior therapy.* New York: Springer, 1997.

Ellis, A., Gordon, J., Neenan, M., & Palmer, S., *Stress counseling.* New York: Springer, 1998.

Ellis, A., & Harper, R.A. *A guide to rational living.* Rev. ed. North Hollywood, CA: Melvin Powers/Wilshire Books, 1997.

Ellis, A., & Harper, R.A. *Dating, mating, and relating. How to build a healthy relationship.* New York: Citadel Press, 2002.

Ellis, A., & Harper, R.A. *How to stop destroying your relationship.* New York: Citadel Press, 2002.

SELECTED REFERENCES

Ellis, A., & MacLaren, C. *Rational emotive behavior therapy: A therapist's guide.* Atascadero, CA: Impact Publishers, 1998.

Ellis, A., & Powers, M.G. *The secret of overcoming verbal abuse.* North Hollywood, CA: Melvin Powers, 2000.

Ellis, A., & Sagarin, E. *Nymphomania: A study of the oversexed woman,* 1973.

Ellis, A., & Tafrate, R. *How to control your anger before it controls you.* New York: Citadel Press, 1998.

Ellis, A., & Velten, E. *When AA doesn't work for you: Rational steps for quitting alcohol.* New York: Barricade Books, 1992.

Ellis, A., & Velten, E. *Optimal aging: Getting over getting older.* Chicago: Open Court, 1998.

Ernike, K. School dress codes vs. a sea of bare flesh. *New York Times:* p. A1, 2001.

Fiske, S. "Sex at School." *Psychology today.* Page 32, 2003.

Freud, S. *Basic writings.* New York: Modern Library, 1938.

Gordon, S. Will today's sexuality become tomorrow's myths? *Journal of child psychology,* pp. 4-5, 1974.

Hellman, P. *Naked at work (and other fears).* New York: New American Library, 2002.

Holstein, L.L. *How to have magnificent sex.* New York: Harmony Books, 2001.

Hooper, A. *Sexopedia.* New York: D.K. Publishing, Inc., 2003.

Hutcherson, H. *What your mother never told you about sex.* New York: G.P. Putnam's Sons, 2002.

Janofsky, M. Defining pornography proves tricky, even in a Utah town. *New York Times,* p. 2, 2003.

Janssen, E., Everaerd, W., Spierling, M., & Janssen, J. Automatic processes and the appraisal of sexual stimuli. *Journal of sex research, 37,* 8-23, 2000.

Kinsey, A.C., Pomeroy, W.B., & Martin, C. *Sexual behavior in the human male.* Philadelphia: Saunders, 1948.

Kinsey, A.C., Pomeroy, W.B., Martin, C., & Bell, A. *Sexual behavior in the human female.* Philadelphia: Saunders, 1953.

Kirkendall, L.A., & Curtis, A. *Premarital intercourse and interpersonal relationships.* New York: Julian, 1961.

Leiblum, S., & Sachs, J. *Getting the sex you want.* New York: Crown, 2002.

Levine, J. *Harmful to minors: The perils of protecting children from sex.* Minneapolis, MN: University of Minnesota Press, 2002.

Locker, S. *The complete idiot's guide to amazing sex.* 2nd edition. Indianapolis, IN: Alpha Books, 2003.

Masters, W.H., & Johnson, V.E. *Human sexual response.* Boston: Houghton Mifflin, 1960.

Masters, W.H., & Johnson, V.E. *Human sexual inadequacy.* Boston: Houghton Mifflin, 1970.

Mosher, C. *Health care without shame.* Emeryville, CA: Greenery Press, 1999.

Moser, C., & Hardy, J. *Sex disasters - and how to survive them.* California: Greenery Press, 2002.

Otto, H. *The new sexuality.* Palo Alto, CA: Science and Behavior Books, 1972.

Peterson, J.R. *365 ways to improve your sex life.* New York: Penguin Books, 1996.

Peterson, James *Playboy's history of the sexual revolution: 1900-1999.* New York: Grove Press, 1999.

Pillay, A.P., & Ellis, A. (Eds.). *Sex, society, and the individual.* Bombay: International Journal of Sexology, 1953.

Redbook *Report on female sexuality.* New York: Redbook Magazine, 1997.

Reiss, I.L. *Premarital sexual standards in America.* Glencoe: Free Press, 1960.

Reiss, I.L. *Solving America's sexual crisis*. Amsterdam, NY: Prometheus Books, 1997.

Reiss, I.L. Sexual attitudes and behavior. In N.J. Smelser & P.B. Bates, *International encyclopedia of the social and behavioral sciences* (Vol. 21, pp. 13969-13973). New York: Elseria Science, 2001.

Russell, B. *Marriage and morals*. New York: Simon & Schuster, 1929.

Salerno, S. (Ed.). *The book of sex*. New York: Berkley Publishing Group, 2001.

Schnarch, D. *Resurrecting sex*. New York: Harper Collins Publishers, 2002.

Shabsigh, R. *Back to great sex*. New York: Kensington Publishers, 2003.

Talbot, M. 6.30.02: The way we live now. *New York Times Magazine*, pp. 11-12, 2002.

Thomas, L.M., & Levin, M.G. *Sexual orientation and human rights*. Walnut Creek, CA: Rowman & Littlefield, 1999.

Tillman-Healy, L.M. *Between gay and straight*. Walnut Creek, CA: Altamira Press, 2001.

Velten, E. Acceptance and construction: rational emotive behavior therapy and homosexuality. In C. Shelley, *Contemporary perspectives on psychotherapy and homosexuality* (pp. 190-221). New York: Free Association, 1998.

Watts, A.W. *Nature man and woman*. New York: New American Library, 1958.

Wolfe, J.L. *What to do when he has a headache*. New York: Hyperion, 1992.

World Association of Sexology. *Declaration of sexual rights*. Geneva: World Association of Sexology, 1999.

About the Author

Albert Ellis, Ph.D., born in Pittsburgh and raised in New York City, holds M.A. and Ph.D. degrees in clinical psychology from Columbia University. He has held many important psychological positions, including Chief Psychologist of the State of New Jersey and adjunct professorships at Rutgers and other universities. He is currently president of the Albert Ellis Institute in New York City; has practiced psychotherapy, marriage and family counseling, and sex therapy for sixty years; and continues this practice at the Psychological Center of the Institute in New York. He is the founder of Rational Emotive Behavior Therapy (REBT), the first of the now popular Cognitive Behavior Therapies (CBT).

Dr. Ellis has served as president of the Division of Consulting Psychology of the American Psychological Association and of the Society for the Scientific Study of Sexuality; and he has also served as officer of several professional societies, including the American Association of Marital and Family Therapy, the American Academy of Psychotherapists, and the American Association of Sex Educators, Counselors, and Therapists. He is a diplomat in clinical psychology of the American Board of Professional Psychology and of several other professional organizations.

Professional societies that have given Dr. Ellis their highest professional and clinical awards include the American Psychological Association, the Association for the Advancement of Behavior Therapy, the American Counseling Association, and the American Psychopathological Association. He was ranked as one of the "most influential psychologists" by both American and Canadian psychologists and counselors. He has served as consulting or associate editor of many scientific journals, and has published over 800 scientific papers and more than 200 audio and video cassettes. He has authored or edited over 70 books and monographs, including a number of best-selling popular and professional volumes. Some of his best-known books include *How to Live With a "Neurotic," The Art and Science of Love, A Guide to Rational Living, Reason and Emotion in Psychotherapy, How to Stubbornly Refuse to Make Yourself Miserable About Anything—Yes, Anything!, Overcoming Procrastination, Overcoming Resistance, The Practice of Rational Emotive Behavior Therapy, How to Make Yourself Happy and Remarkably Less Disturbable, Feeling Better, Getting Better, Staying Better, Overcoming Destructive Beliefs, Feelings, and Behaviors,* and *Anger: How to Live With It and Without It.*